# JONATHAN WHISTMAN

# THE
# SALES BOSS

## THE REAL SECRET
## TO HIRING, TRAINING,
## AND MANAGING
## A SALES TEAM

REVENUE

IDEAS

PROBLEM SOLVING

CHANGE

YES

DISC

NEGOTIATE

TEAM

AUTHENTIC

IDEAS

TRUSTED

WILEY

Published by John Wiley & Sons, Inc., Hoboken, New Jersey
Published simultaneously in Canada

For general information about our other products and services, please contact our Customer Care Department within the United States at (800) 762-2974, outside the United States at (317) 572-3993 or fax (317) 572-4002.

Wiley publishes in a variety of print and electronic formats and by print-on-demand. Some material included with standard print versions of this book may not be included in e-books or in print-on-demand. If this book refers to media such as a CD or DVD that is not included in the version you purchased, you may download this material at http://booksupport.wiley.com. For more information about Wiley products, visit www.wiley.com.

**Library of Congress Cataloging-in-Publication Data:**
Names: Whistman, Jonathan, author.
Title: The sales boss : the real secret to hiring, training and managing a
  sales team / Jonathan Whistman.
Description: Hoboken : Wiley, 2016. | Includes bibliographical references and
  index.
Identifiers: LCCN 2016013235 (print) | LCCN 2016023020 (ebook) | ISBN
  9781119286646 (hardback) | ISBN 9781119286721 (pdf) | ISBN
  9781119286745 (epub)
Subjects: LCSH: Sales management. | Employee selection. | Employees—Training
  of.
Classification: LCC HF5438.4 .W45 2016 (print) | LCC HF5438.4 (ebook) | DDC
  658.8/102—dc23
LC record available at https://lccn.loc.gov/2016013235

10 9 8 7 6 5 4 3 2 1

# Contents

*Foreword*                                                                                    *v*

*Introduction*                                                                                *ix*


**Chapter  1**   The Work of a Sales Boss                                    1

**Chapter  2**   The Importance of Sacred Rhythms                  9

**Chapter  3**   The DNA of a Sales Boss                                 15

What It Takes to Be Great                                                        17

The Management Code                                                            22

**Chapter  4**   The Truth About Humans                                29

Five Fundamental Truths About Human Behavior   32

A Unique Insider Language                                                    40

Rituals                                                                                     41

Having a Common Enemy                                                      42

**Chapter  5**   Your First 30 Days as Boss                               45

Getting Started with Your Team:
The First 30 Days                                                                   49

**Chapter  6**   Understanding the Market for Hiring             69

Why Hiring a Superstar Salesperson Is Tough           71

**Chapter  7**   Step by Step to Hiring a Sales Superstar        77

The Selection Process                                                             79

The Four-Stage Interview Process                                       89

**Chapter 8**  Use the Power of Science in Selection        103

**Chapter 9**  On-Boarding a New Member of the
Sales Team                                                 109

**Chapter 10**  Know Your Sales Process and
Your Numbers                                               123
The Numbers That Matter                                    129

**Chapter 11**  Who Gets My Time and Attention?            135

**Chapter 12**  Team Rhythms That Lead to Group
Cohesion                                                   141
Group Meetings                                             145

**Chapter 13**  Individual Rhythms That Lead to Star
Performances                                               153
Individual Meetings Framework                              155
Three Types of Individual Meetings                         158

**Chapter 14**  Keep Score Publicly; Motivate Individually  181

**Chapter 15**  Lead by Principle, Not Policy              189

**Chapter 16**  Make Sales Technology Work for You         195

**Chapter 17**  Money Talks: Compensation Planning         205
Base Salary                                                210
Variable Commissions                                       211
Bonuses                                                    211

**Chapter 18**  Forecasting the Future                     219

**Chapter 19**  Replicating Success                        225

**Chapter 20**  The Business of You                        233

*The Sales Boss Scorecard*                                 *243*
*The Scorecard*                                            *243*
*About the Author*                                         *254*
*Index*                                                    *256*

# Foreword

I am pleased to be introducing you to the book you hold in your hands, *The Sales Boss: The Real Secret to Hiring, Training, and Managing a Sales Team*, as I have experienced first-hand the financial results possible when an organization's sales team is led by a skilled person operating at the highest level of sales management. My hope is that after you read the book you'll understand all of the nuances involved in leading a high performance sales team and that you'll agree with the statement *Nothing happens until someone sells something*. This is a statement I only fully understood after leading and being responsible for creating profit at for-profit organizations and a lesson I believe is critical to pass on to leaders at today's companies. I'd like to briefly share my journey on the path to understanding the truth behind this statement.

Starting my corporate career as an industrial engineer working on the manufacturing line of a GE plant in Middle America, I could have sworn then that *nothing happened if someone didn't make something*. I quickly learned, however, that a person or a business can make anything it wants, at whatever quality level it chooses, and price it however it sees fit. But there is simply no guarantee that it will sell. And if it doesn't sell, then there is no business . . . period.

After a few years of working on the line, I decided to continue my education and was accepted into Harvard Business School's MBA program. Over the next years, I rubbed shoulders with the global business elite and the who's who of management academia, including the likes of Michael Porter. The interesting thing was, though, that while we spent a lot of time learning about strategy, leadership, and even marketing, neither sales nor sales management was ever discussed.

It wasn't until I went back to corporate America as a marketing manager in a medical equipment business that I began to realize that *sales* was likely the most important function never taught in business school.

In my new role, I noticed a great deal of management time and financial investment being devoted to managing our customers' increasingly professionalized purchasing function. From better selling techniques that refocused our sales force's efforts from feature/benefit-based to value-based selling, all the way through significant investments in sales automation technology, the amount of energy and resources being pumped into better selling was hard to miss.

Even so, only a few teams and individuals met their increasingly challenging goals. Even fewer exceeded them. One thing, however, was common among those individuals and teams that were consistent top performers: They were led by a remarkable sales manager. The old adage noting that there are indeed no bad soldiers, only bad officers, began to prove itself over and over, every year that I observed what made top performance in sales happen.

Patterns quickly became obvious in those sales leaders who were consistent in their results. They were individuals who seemed to have a special kind of rapport with their teams and who made no excuses. When I asked their team members what made their managers successful, the answers I received were almost always consistent:

> "We know what they expect, and we are happy to consistently hear about it."
>
> "With [insert manager name here], every week we have to show up and answer the same questions, and our answers better be right."
>
> "I want to be the best, so I want to work under the best."
>
> "XYZ is about as maniacal about our rhythm and cadence as he is about being accurate in our forecast."

There were other answers that I did not expect, however. They were more subtle distinctions in how these managers operated. But, as I quickly learned, those subtleties made a huge difference in results:

> "We know our manager has our backs and cares about us."
>
> "They always take full responsibility for our results. We always want to make them look good, because they make us good."
>
> "They make me a better person."

Nothing really magical came up, however. No especially noticeable skill or interpersonal characteristic such as an unusually high level of charisma ever reared its head. This made it clear to me that, much like every other function in business, sales leadership is much less art and much more science. It is a process and, as such, has recognizable variables that, when managed and controlled for appropriately, produce consistent results.

Over the last decade, I've spent a large portion of my professional time learning about these variables from more than a dozen experts and consultants. I've even been personally trained and certified in well-known selling methodologies, including Miller Heiman's Strategic Selling and SPIN, to further develop my own selling and sales management skills. It has been time well spent. My companies' results have always spoken for themselves.

This is how I originally came across Jonathan Whistman and his Sales Boss framework. Based on the results we achieved, Jonathan has trained several of our teams, and his company evaluates all of our employees before they are hired. So I was delighted to read this book, as it provides readers with a framework to recognize all of the key variables that I've identified over the years as being "the difference that makes a difference."

It offers great potential to progressive organizations and individuals who are listeners and learners, not sandbaggers. I have used its concepts at every one of my companies, and they work. Most importantly, however, the framework elegantly highlights the fact that selling is not a stand-alone process. To borrow from Churchill, it only represents the end of the beginning. I encourage you to read with an open mind and be ready for the transformation into a Sales Boss.

Ruben Salinas<br>
President and CEO<br>
Parsagen Diagnostics, Inc.

# Introduction

If you have ever been on the inside of a top-performing sales team, you know it can look like magic to an outsider. The revenue piles up, in what seems like an effortless process. Everyone—vendors, suppliers, marketing prospects, customers, management, and the sales team—is entwined in an elegant dance, the result of which is increasing revenue. The truth is, it only looks magical.

It is the result of a carefully orchestrated plan. My belief is that at the center of that successful plan is the *sales manager*. If the company is underperforming, it is always the sales manager. Unfortunately, the opposite isn't always the truth. If a company *is* performing well, it is not always the result of the sales manager! I know this seems like a harsh view.

If you are the sales manager, you get the blame when things go wrong and only partial credit when things go well. I'd suggest you get used to it, as that's the reality in every company and if you are to succeed you must be up to this challenge. You must believe that if things are not going right, you and only you are to blame.

- If the marketing department isn't getting the message out correctly in the right places or with the right tone, it's your fault.

- If the customer service department is failing to deliver great service and your company's reputation is suffering as a result, it's your fault.
- If your company's product is out of date and not meeting the current needs of the market, it's your fault.
- If your company doesn't pay enough to be competitive, it's your fault.
- If your company isn't [insert anything here], it's your fault.

The power of taking full responsibility for your company's results cannot be understated. It is critical. If you can't adopt this mindset, save everyone a bit of trouble and get out while you still can. You will never deliver results at the highest level. There are much easier ways to make a living than managing a sales team. The rewards are great, but so is the task at hand. In fact, I call the sales manager operating at the highest level the Sales Boss. The Boss isn't content to manage. The Boss gets results. In this book you will find the real secrets to hiring, managing, and training a sales team.

While I recommend reading the entire book for a full overview on all of the key components to being a great Sales Boss, you might also choose to move directly to the chapters on topics that you know you currently need help with as you build your team. Realize though that best results come from an application of all of the concepts presented in this book working in concert together. This is the secret. Why should you heed the advice in this book? Primarily, because it works. I've built, operated, and sold a number of companies that all depended on the ability to sell and build a sales team. I've "eaten my own dog food," to borrow a phrase. I've kept a sales journal and recorded my personal sales metrics daily for the last 20 years.

I am writing this book after having worked directly with sales teams as a sales consultant for the last 15 years, working with some of the top brands in each niche. I have personally observed over 2,500 individual sales calls and participated in the coaching and training of these salespeople. I've attended many hundreds of sales meetings and observed the skills and abilities of the managers running these meetings and also helped them develop their coaching and management skills.

I can tell you that I have seen some of the best coaching and selling in the world, and I've also had a front-row seat to some of the worst. I'll be able to give you real-world examples of both and share the impact that each has on the performance of a team. This knowledge doesn't come from academia. It comes from having been involved on the front lines of management.

While working with my clients, I have had the opportunity to look behind the curtain at these companies and see how they utilize their customer relationship management (CRM) systems, how they develop their sales funnels and marketing, and how they approach the hiring, training, and on-boarding of new salespeople. I've seen how companies struggle to implement tracking systems and get the team to use them, and then how the team reacts to various tactics to get them to utilize a system. I'll share these insights.

Outside of the business arena and prior to my work with sales teams, I was deeply involved in a religious cult, being raised inside the group from birth and breaking free from its control as a young adult. I won't go into the details, as that would be another book entirely!

So why do I mention this detail of my life here? Despite all of the wrongs of the cult, it did give me an insight into how people's beliefs about themselves and their environment can be shaped. I was able to witness the power of belief in the daily actions of people. I learned how to overcome and change deeply held habits—not only my own, but also those of the people in my group. The cult was a gigantic laboratory of human nature. I learned a lot about motivation tools outside of money or the threat of unemployment, as the entire group, including the leadership team, were volunteers who chose to be involved.

I spent over 10,000 hours voluntarily knocking on people's doors and giving them the cult's sales pitch. I also recruited, trained, and mentored many others to do the same. I spent many thousands more hours in one-on-one coaching sessions.

In many ways, building these "religious sales teams" and managing their activity was much harder than building a team for a company. I wasn't paid, and neither did I have any money to offer converts. To join the Cult Team, you'd be an unpaid volunteer, give up many of your family and friends, and live as an outsider! This was not an easy sell, but I admit I had a pretty good conversion rate! Many of the lessons I learned as I witnessed human nature have shaped the insights I have utilized in helping companies find, train, coach, and mentor a top-performing sales team. While I rejected the teachings of the cult, I believe this experience has given me some unique insights into what it takes to create a winning sales team or to turn an underperforming one around.

In this book, I will describe all of the key areas that a Sales Boss should be focused on in performing at the highest level and building the best team. First and foremost, if you want to have a superstar sales team that wins consistently and demolishes the competition, then YOU as the sales manager must be a superstar. No superstar works for an average boss for long. Are you a little fluffy? Or are you game-ready? We'll look at mindsets and specific actions that must be taken consistently for top results.

As you read, mark up the pages identifying the ideas that you can apply. When you read something familiar, the question should not be "Have I heard this before?" It should be "How good have I been at applying this?" When you read something new or something that you might initially disagree with, ask yourself: "What would this mean to my results if it were indeed true?" You might also ask: "What makes me disagree with this statement?" Perhaps you'll discover that it is some past experience with a previous manager or your personality preference that is causing you to dismiss the suggestion.

I would recommend that before you dismiss an idea or thought I've presented here you fully understand the "why" behind your dismissal. I know that not all of the thoughts I've presented here will serve every manager in every type of company in every situation. I do know, however, that what I will describe works when skillfully applied. I won't have accomplished my goal unless something in these pages makes you uncomfortable or makes you acknowledge that you could be better than you are today as a leader of your team. I believe that real change only happens with a bit of discomfort. In some instances, I will give you actual wording and phrasing so that you can visualize yourself having effective conversations with the people on your team. Adapt the phrasing to suit your personality, but first make sure you understand the impact the words are intended to have as you craft your unique style.

As you take on the role of the Sales Boss, you will be leading the sales team, but remember which team you are on. You are a member of the management team. You can't just be "one of the guys" on the sales team. A good relationship with every department head and other managers will be essential to achieving the best results. Because tools utilized in the field of sales change rapidly and to offer you additional resources, we've created a place for you to download these tools. Please take a moment to register at www.jonathanwhistman.com/thesalesboss.

Let's get started.

# The Importance of Sacred Rhythms

I love jazz and think the jazz club is a perfect metaphor for a top-performing sales culture. Think about what happens when you enter a great jazz club. In fact, imagine going to the club after a hard day's work when you aren't in the mood to have a good time. What happens? Isn't it true that before long you are tapping your foot to the rhythm? Pretty soon your body starts to sway, a smile lights up your face, and as you look around the room, everyone is moving in time to the music. Usually you end up staying longer than you intended!

What's happened? The rhythm has infected you and you can't resist. The beat tells you what's happening and pulls you along for the ride. The beat also informed the members of the band of the structure, and so a great jazz ensemble can allow an individual musician to riff over the top of the beat, adding his individual gift of expression, and then land back with the rest of the musicians right on the beat. As the musician takes off on his journey of notes, you can feel the rest of the musicians falling in line behind to support the beauty, and the audience relishes each surprising note. A great performance always takes you on a journey, even when you enter the club "not in the mood."

This is what you are striving for when you build a great sales culture. You create an environment with enough motivational power that when a new member joins the team he or she is infected with the rhythm of your team and can't resist getting in sync with the group. It is almost effortless. New members can express their unique talents "riffing" over the top and adding their gifts, but in the end landing right on the beat of the team. The rest of the company supports them and effortlessly integrates them into the team's successes. You create an environment that carries even the seasoned salespeople through the times when they are not in the mood to perform at their best. Does this describe your sales culture today? Or are you more like a grade school band struggling to find the beat?

I've seen sales organizations that have rhythm, and you can see the transformative effect it has on people. I was interviewing a saleswoman inside of one such company and she said with excitement: "There is an energy inside the building as the month draws to a close. Everyone just seems alive with the certainty that we'll exceed the sales target, just as we do every month. You can't walk through the halls without noticing the tempo." That's magic.

If you were to walk through the halls of this company, you'd notice large TV screens with all of their sales results by individuals being continually updated for everyone to see. You would find screens that highlight which customers they'd recently lost to competitors and who were on a win-back list. This team didn't like to lose, and they didn't often lose as a result.

Imagine walking into this company as a new salesperson. What would you be thinking? You would instantly know that you were about to play on a great team and would perform better as a result. Any smugness you had about being a star player at your last company would disappear in your desire to prove that you deserve a spot on this A-team. This is the environment you will design for your team when you are a Sales Boss. It makes everything easier.

It's all in the rhythm. What rhythms have you established for your team that inform them about how the game is played at your company? A great Sales Boss has well-established "Sacred Rhythms."

What do I mean by sacred? One typically thinks of sacred in a religious context, but the word means that we hold something as highly valued, deserving of respect or devotion. To have Sacred Rhythms within your sales department, you must have established rituals that the team can depend on to be used consistently. We'll talk throughout this book about what some of the rhythms might be. For instance, your monthly, weekly, and daily communications with your team form the foundational rhythm. The format and expectations of what happens during these meetings become another rhythm. Your team comes to depend on this rhythm for informing them what the beat is of your company and how they sync up with it.

Here is a challenge I see in many underperforming teams: The manager doesn't have any rhythm! The manager will put a monthly meeting on the schedule, but a few days before will move the meeting for some unexpected travel or another event. Pretty soon the monthly meeting is a quarterly meeting, and this sloppiness seeps into every aspect of the sales team. The weekly coaching sessions become weakly done sessions, if conducted at all. There is no excitement in the halls and no cause for celebration. The month ends as though the team has been running on a treadmill set one setting higher than they can sustain and then, just as they get to the end, they start a new month already drained.

The sales manager makes bad hiring decisions. Sales roles are filled, and then the people are let go, impacting the cohesiveness of the team and sucking out the willingness of the team to get behind the next new salesperson. As a result, the rest of the company treats any new hire with a "wait-and-see" attitude before jumping in to help the person be successful. The manager loses any credibility. That's not magic. It's the kiss of death—indeed, a slow painful death. A Sales Boss doesn't have that problem.

You are responsible for the energy, music, and rhythms in your jazz club. Would they make you want to dance and stay longer than you intended? Developing Sacred Rhythms means that you decide what needs to happen and that those items are sacred. They don't move, alter, or change. Your team understands that's the way it happens. They understand the beat, and they start to depend on it.

Not everything can be sacred; you'll need some flexibility. But some things must be highly valued, deserving of respect and devotion, or nothing will be. Your role as manager is to decide what is sacred and communicate that clearly to your team. I'll be offering some suggestions within the pages of this book, and you will want to pick the ones most important to you for the stage of development of your team.

Before we move on, how would you rate your rhythm? Better yet, how would your team rate your rhythm?

# The DNA of a Sales Boss

# What It Takes to Be Great

The path to becoming the sales manager in most organizations is familiar. Typically, a particular salesperson is the top performer, and so he or she is promoted to the manager role. Sometimes this works, but more often than not you will find that the newly promoted manager struggles. Some of the very things that made the person a great salesperson stand in the way of him or her excelling in the role of manager.

What makes a great Sales Boss? This is not an easy question to answer since on the surface many different personality styles succeed, but I have found some key DNA that it seems the best Bosses all possess.

## 1. They have been in a sales role, but usually not as the top performer on that team if the team was composed of high performers

Why is this? In sales, there are always some very high earners whose success in sales defies any checklist or traits that might be taught. They are, to use a cliché, "born to be a salesperson." I call them the Awesome Anomaly. While nice to have on your sales team, they make terrible managers. To them, sales are effortless and unexplainable. These are usually the ones who have been best managed by the manager staying out of the way and letting them work their magic. In some cases I have seen these high-earners be the very ones you might think least likely to have success, but nonetheless close sales month in and month out like clockwork. The problem is that if you make them into sales managers, they can't teach someone else how to do what they do. They've never struggled. It has always come easily to them. They have never had to become students of selling and adopt new and creative, perhaps counterintuitive, ways of selling. When push comes to shove, they'll rescue the new salesperson on the team by closing the business for her rather than teaching her a lasting skill. These high-earner Awesome Anomalies, the naturally talented salespeople, will typically shy away from any management duties, viewing any effort at managing the team as micromanagement, because they felt similarly about anyone who tried to manage them in the past. They'll end up being miserable in the process, and their effectiveness as salespeople will also be ruined. It is better to keep them as the wise sages on the team to whom you can turn for insights into your sales process and customers, rather than promote them into the management role.

Sometimes, despite knowing the low chance of success, a company is tempted to "try them out" in the management role thinking they can always be moved back into the sales role if it doesn't work out. This is never a successful plan. Once you have moved an Awesome Anomaly into the sales management role, this person's ego will now see him- or herself as a manager. If you require anyone to move back into a sales role, this will be seen as a demotion or a failure. The Awesome Anomaly isn't used to failure; he or she's been awesome forever. These people either resent you when you force the issue or more likely will move on to another company (your competition) as an Awesome Anomaly salesperson. This is not the outcome you want.

The best manager is one who has had success in selling, but usually not as the top person on the team. This person is credible with a sales team because he or she has been there and understands the fears, the emotions, and the reality of the sales world. These people experienced the pressures of being required to carry a quota. Unlike the Awesome Anomaly, because they

- Believe bigger
- Believe the fault is yours

When faced with a decision or planning something with your team and when evaluating your own performance, use the code to make sure you are staying on the most effective path to success. Let's look at these in more detail.

## Don't micro-manage; be actively engaged

There is perhaps no more derisive term to explain someone's management style than calling him or her a "micro-manager." However, the term micro-manager actually has a fairly wide range of meanings. Typically, micro-manager is a label people use to describe a manager who is so involved in the small details that the talent of the individual employee is constrained and the environment becomes oppressive. It is that definition that I refer to when I say, "Don't micro-manage; be actively engaged." In their desire not to be labeled as micro-managers, you will see sales managers who are so far removed from the details that they can't realistically expect to have an impact on the results happening in the field. The Sales Boss is not that way. The Management Code requires that you be actively engaged and understand the details of the world your salespeople are operating in. A Sales Boss wants to know even the small nuances. The key difference is that it comes from a place of curiosity and engagement, not from a desire to control or give an opinion on each detail. You might think of it as when a parent asks a child what she did that day and asks great questions because the parent is curious and engaged, rather than asking out of fear that the child is involved in some mischief! If in the process of being curious the parent discovers something that requires intervention, then he or she certainly does something, but the parent isn't initiating the involvement purely with the thought of control.

A word of caution: Don't let your view of how well you are following the Management Code be impacted by the underperforming salesperson. Don't let salespeople guilt you into thinking you are micro-managing when you are merely applying strategic pressure. My son always said he had cleaned his room until I announced it was inspection time and then suddenly his definition of a clean room started to change. You will likewise need to do a certain amount of inspection of what your salespeople tell you they are doing. This is not micro-management. Underperformers usually have learned that they can hurl the accusation of "micro-manager" at a boss and that the boss will back off and alleviate some of the pressure. Be fully aware of why you are involved, and don't lessen pressure under an accusation of micro-management.

## Honesty always; no one should ever be surprised

Nothing violates our trust as much as someone being dishonest with us. You should always strive to be as honest as possible when you are dealing with your salespeople. When I say "as possible," I recognize that sometimes things happen in a company that are not appropriate to share openly. When this is the case, you still should try to be as open and honest as you can, and at least acknowledge to the salesperson when there are things you can't discuss and try to share the "why." The Sales Boss should never try to make the sales numbers look better than they are. If there is bad news, share it quickly. Bad news is not like fine wine. It doesn't get better with age. As you start to formulate ideas or opinions or take a course of action, begin to prepare the minds and hearts of the people around you. They should never be surprised. If someone's performance is poor, you must have had conversations about it.

## Be authentic; people are people

We are drawn to authenticity, and it is the same for the people we lead. Authenticity requires that you be open about who you are and what your agenda is. An authentic person doesn't put on airs or have a desire to gain credit or admiration from people under false pretenses. You don't have to be right or perfect or have all of the answers. If you can be vulnerable with people, it will go a long way toward causing them to trust you and follow you. This means recognizing that people are human and won't always reach the level of performance that we'd consider ideal. Although we work to get the best from others and from ourselves, an authentic person sees the whole of other people and recognizes that they have lives outside of work. You don't want to just be seen as "the Boss," but as a multifaceted human being who authentically cares about the lives of the people on your team.

## Be the thermostat, not the thermometer

The Management Code requires that you recognize that you are ultimately responsible for the team's attitude, mentality, and results. If you don't like what is happening, it is a reflection of you, not the team. A thermostat sets the desired temperature in a room, and the temperature gradually raises or lowers to that set point. A thermometer, on the other hand, simply tells you what the temperature currently is. A Sales Boss (and in fact any manager) enters the environment and people adjust to his or her presence. If you have a negative attitude or outlook, the team will soon adjust to hold that same view. You must have confidence in the team and be enthusiastic about even the most difficult of challenges. You must believe in your team before they can believe in themselves.

When you need a break, you need to take it away from a place where the team will be negatively impacted. When you are with the team, be the thermostat. If your role becomes one of simply reporting the sales results to the rest of the management team, then you are the thermometer and you will soon be replaced as redundant. In sales we often hear the term "move the needle" used in reference to increasing sales. If you want to be the Sales Boss, get in the habit of thinking of the needle on a thermostat and then reflect on what you are doing to control the temperature of the environment that surrounds your team.

## Trust and expect the best, but verify

The phrase "trust but verify" was adopted and popularized by the American president Ronald Reagan. It was actually taught to him by Suzanne Massie, a writer on Russia. She taught him the Russian proverb, "doverya no proveryai," meaning "trust but verify." President Reagan used this phrase often in the time period after learning it to emphasize the extensive verification procedures that would enable both Russia and the United States to feel comfortable that treaties were being complied with. A Sales Boss should also be fond of this axiom. Your team should know that you trust them and take them at their word; however, you will also look for verification. Here is where routines and expectations can really help. If you have established Sacred Rhythms, then the team will expect that you will inspect what you expect. They'll know that things are verified. It will be a part of the fabric of how things are done. If, however, you only verify after you suspect that things aren't being done correctly, then you risk damaging your relationship with your team. We'll talk about performance metrics in Chapter 10, and this will serve as a good example of "trust but verify." If your team has the expectation of a certain number of field visits per week being made by each salesperson, then they can also expect that you'll be looking for evidence of these visits in the call reports, hotel receipts, or other places. Trust, but verify.

## Believe bigger

You should always try to believe bigger than the team. Create compelling visions not only for the company but also for the performance of each individual. In almost no other role is the need for believing bigger as important as for the Sales Boss. You are considered a success when the company grows its market share and revenues. Always have a bigger mindset. When talking about mundane types of things, try to connect them to something bigger. For instance, what impact does your product have on your customers? I do sales consulting. I help companies sell more stuff. To be honest, that isn't very exciting by itself, but because I believe bigger I stay motivated and my team stays focused. I choose to believe that when I teach someone to be a better Sales Boss I am helping fathers and mothers to be able to provide a better quality of life for their children. I believe that people who are high earners have the freedom to donate to worthy causes, such as finding a cure for cancer, or eradicating illiteracy, in a bigger way. When I do my best work, the world changes as a result. What happens when your team does its job? Believe bigger.

## Believe the fault is yours

Accepting fault when things go wrong is always the right thing to do. To use a well-worn phrase: "The buck stops here." Even if the problem is outside of your direct area of control, the Management Code requires you to accept fault. By accepting fault, you are in a position to do something about it. When your team comes under fire from another area of the company, accept full responsibility. Your team should never hear you pass the fault on to them. These simple words, "It's my fault, I should have . . .," will help you impact results while keeping the trust of your team. Sometimes it will require extreme humility and you'll want to blame someone else for outcomes. Remember that a Sales Boss believes that it is all within his or her control and thus always accepts fault. It's a mindset of power.

• • •

Take a moment to review what you have just learned regarding the DNA of a Sales Boss and the Management Code. How well do you currently do in each of these areas? We'll spend a lot of time in the remainder of the book focused on understanding and developing other people. Your effectiveness with others will be more greatly impacted by how well you do with yourself than with any of the other areas we will cover. I find that sometimes people will self-rate themselves better than they deserve. It's a human tendency, after all. If we thought there was an issue, we would most likely have already worked on it. Ask people you trust for feedback, specifically as it relates to the points in this chapter. You'll receive better feedback if you give people permission to be honest.

# 4

# The Truth About Humans

## 3. People love autopilot

Have you ever been on a road you've traveled many times before and arrived at your destination safely only to realize you can't remember any details of the trip? You can't remember stopping at any of the lights, merging into traffic, or anything really, but somehow you've made it to your destination? If so, you understand autopilot. As humans, we have the unique and amazing ability to do even complex things on autopilot. In fact, this usually serves us well so our minds aren't tasked with thousands of little decisions, but can think about other things.

Here is the challenge: Not all of actions we have on autopilot serve us well. As managers, we can start executing our jobs on autopilot. Your meetings, emails, phone calls, and pipeline reviews can all be done without thought. Our salespeople can likewise run their sales activity on autopilot.

People love autopilot. A Sales Boss will understand this and leverage autopilot to help many of the functions of the team happen without much thought or intervention. This is why Sacred Rhythms have such power to influence results. On the other side of the coin, a Sales Boss must avoid being on autopilot when involved in key critical activities. A Sales Boss recognizes when a team member is operating on autopilot but is off course and requires an intervention.

## 4. People need to belong

We instinctively know people need to belong. The difference between a manager and a Sales Boss is that the Sales Boss knows how to craft an environment in which people want to belong and where belonging has the added benefit of making people perform at a higher level than they would otherwise. People adjust their behavior to fit the norms of the group they want to belong to. This adjustment happens without thought, and you can use it to your advantage. Rather than needing to be present to enforce the norms of the group, you can craft an environment that reinforces your expectations for you.

As an example, imagine that you are at a sports venue and you head into the bathroom. I know this is not a pleasant thought and I apologize, but hang with me for a minute. When you wash your hands and use the paper towel, you'll likely find yourself shooting the towel for the wastebasket and trying not to touch anything on your way out! What happens if you miss? Not a big deal right? You would probably just let the missed shot lie there on the floor.

Now, let's change the environment. Let's say you are heading for the restroom at a five-star restaurant. Isn't it true that you are much more careful when you wash up? If you splash water on the counter, you might even use your towel to tidy it up, and my guess is it never even crosses your mind to shoot a basket! You adjusted your behavior and standard based on the norms of the group you wanted to be accepted by at the time.

Your team will behave and adjust in a similar manner.

## 5. The only reasons that matter are their reasons

This insight is the final truth I'll mention, but it is perhaps the most powerful. We must understand why people on our team show up and work. The only reasons that matter are *their* reasons.

- Do they want a promotion?
- Do they want the experience to move to another company or role?
- Do they need increased income to get out of debt?
- Are they worried about retirement or college?
- Is there a hobby to pursue or vacation they want to take?
- Do they have family obligations?

- Is it ego-driven?
- Was this job just the best of several bad options?
- What is the "why" that is driving them at the moment?

Understand their reasons, and then make them your reasons and you'll have the ability to achieve great results. People know when we are in it for ourselves or when we genuinely care about them. Here is a mindset I challenge you to adopt: Care more about the personal success of each member of your sales team than you care about the company's goals. The beauty is that when the personal goals of your team members are met, the company's goals are also met. The difference is where we start the conversation when coaching. For instance, if the salesperson hasn't hit his sales targets, I can either start talking about the company's need, the company's metrics, the company's whatever . . . or I can start the discussion with how this failure is impacting the goals he has regarding retirement, college, or some other aspect that is important to him. We'll discuss coaching in more depth later. For now, it's simply important to remember these five fundamental truths about humans:

1. Things are only good or bad by comparison.
2. People are already giving 100 percent of what they believe they are capable of or they have a reason they believe is valid for not doing so.
3. People love autopilot.
4. People need to belong.
5. The only reasons that matter are their reasons.

No matter whether it is a family, a sports team, a religion, a cult, or a business team, there are always three aspects that maximize a person's feeling of belonging: a unique insider language, rituals, and having a common enemy. Let's consider each of these.

## A Unique Insider Language

Every group has a language that is particular to that group. It might include acronyms only understood if you are in the industry, a team cheer or fight song, or certain behaviors. There are always language cues that tell people they are in the group. In the cult I grew up in, they wouldn't use the typical religious language of churches: salvation, grace, penance, etc. They had their unique labels for these concepts. You could instantly identify other people who were part of the group simply by their use of the proper group language. Inside industries, you'll find acronyms for just about everything, and usually only people "from the industry" understand this language.

What areas of language are unique to your team? Do you understand the subtle bonding power of labeling things in a unique way that identifies your company or team? While you don't want to use acronyms and insider language with prospects who may feel left out when they don't know the meaning, you do want to use such language inside the company. I've seen companies use this principle when they name the types of meetings they hold as a group or when they label their traditions. One company even names the conference areas and walkways on the campus of their company for historical events related to the company or after influential people who have played an important role in shaping the company. You become an insider as you learn the language and reasons for it. It adds significance to belonging.

One of my previous companies had the pattern of having fun-time activities with the whole team on Friday afternoons. We found this led to creativity and a close bond between employees. In keeping with the idea of having a unique insider language, we had fun naming this tradition. We started calling it Fractivity, molding the words Friday and activity together. It became a part of the language and culture. In fact, the marketing team even took it upon themselves to create fun graphic posters each week giving clues to what the Fractivity would be about: chair races, board games, building egg safety harnesses to protect eggs dropped from the rooftop, and other fun activities. These activities increased the sense of belonging and, even years later, if you use the word Fractivity with former employees their eyes will light up, smiles cross their faces, and a story is shared. As a manager, look for areas to create a unique and common language.

At a boy's home for juvenile delinquents that I worked with, the newer students are taught the norms of the group by the older students saying "Around here we . . ." followed by the norm, such as, "don't wear saggy pants" or "ask permission to leave the table." The "around here" becomes a part of the language culture that signals how someone starts to belong, and within a short period of time the new student usually would adjust his behavior and his language so that he belonged. You can see this same phenomenon when you look at gang culture, where a language and the symbols of that language have a unique insider significance.

## Rituals

The most powerful sense of belonging comes from rituals. Think of holidays that mark family or religious tradition and the emotional tie that comes from the accumulation of experiences at these rituals. Understanding the rituals of an organization tells people they belong and that they are home.

What are the rituals of your team? Even small things such as the way you start a meeting or hold a company celebration can have an impact. For instance, at Amazon Fulfillment Centers each meeting is started with the sharing of a safety tip. You'd know that if you belonged! Or at the corporate level each meeting is started with the distribution of a one-page topic summary that is read silently by those in attendance before the start of the meeting discussion. These are all rituals. Knowing and experiencing them increases the sense of belonging.

In one sales organization, the weekly sales meeting starts unprompted by a check-in that rolls through the group: One person simply starts by stating: "Last week I committed to $$ sales and I ended the week at $." The next closest person in the room goes next, with no comment on the previous person's check-in: "Last week I committed to $ sales and I ended the week at $$." This check-in continues until it gets all the way around the room with each salesperson reporting. When everyone has reported in, the manager starts the meeting. This ritual check-in tells people they belong and reinforces the company's belief that numbers matter.

In another company, team members were taught to walk the halls and say "hello" to everyone when they first arrived at the office each day and again when leaving to say "goodnight." Nobody would ever dream of just arriving and locking himself in his office all day. Walking the halls and saying hello became a habit and ritual that created a unique sense of belonging and a culture of human kindness.

You can decide what rituals your team will have. If you spend some time and intention on this, you will create rituals that teach and reinforce while filling the powerful need for people to belong.

## Having a Common Enemy

In sports, it might be the other team and, in business, another company. Nothing gives a more powerful sense of belonging or purpose than having an enemy. Give your team something or someone to fight against and they'll work harder and with more skill. It is a proven fact that nothing bonds a group or people more quickly than being *against* something. It is even more powerful than being *for* something. A wise sales manager understands the power of people's need to belong and uses this need to accomplish the other goals of the organization. Who or what is your team's enemy? How good are you at describing that enemy?

John Legere, T-Mobile's CEO, is an extreme example of this. Known as the "bad boy of telecom," he is often outspoken, calling his competitors "lame" and engaging in public Twitter battles with his competitors such as Sprint's CEO Marcelo Claure. When he took over a failing T-Mobile, he even changed his previous corporate buttoned-up look of a suit and tie and became famous for dressing more like a rock star in pink shirts, leather jackets, and chains. He took to calling his company the "un-carrier" and publicly berating the other companies' sales tactics as unfair to the consumer. He declared war on his rivals. T-Mobile would be different. This was a calculated choice he made to produce outsized results and get the attention from media, shareholders, and his employees that would be needed to produce an increase in revenue.

T-Mobile's market share grew dramatically as a result. In fact, in a single quarter of 2015, he added 2.5 million subscribers in a very crowded marketplace and grew 14 percent more than any of his competition did. Another result of his battle plan was that people who identified themselves as rebels joined his sales team and worked hard to defeat the enemy. Those who wanted to be corporate buttoned-up didn't join the team.

Steve Jobs also understood the concept of an enemy or fostering an us-versus-them mentality. Think of his famous commercials depicting a PC and a Mac as people with personalities. He depicted the PC as old, rigid, and boring, while the Mac was always cool. These commercials were some of the most successful ever, but Steve didn't just limit this concept to commercials.

He brought that same sense of Apple being different to all aspects of his company. People wanted to belong to Apple.

Look at your competitors. Do you look, sound, and feel to your employees as the same thing? If you were in a booth side-by-side at a tradeshow with your competitor, would it be hard to differentiate you? If so, you haven't tapped into the power of the human desire to fight hard against an enemy. How can you define yourself as different and the competition as the enemy?

# 5

# Your First 30 Days as Boss

With the frameworks from Chapter 4 in mind, let's discuss how to get started with your new team. I will make the assumption that you are taking over as the boss of an existing team that needs to be improved. Perhaps you were promoted from within and are now managing a team you once were a part of. This change in position can be tricky! If you've been the sales manager for a while, but haven't been getting fantastic results and you are reading this book, I would suggest the same series of actions, just treat today as day one of your job. Forget the past. If you've been on the team for a while, just preface the actions discussed here with the words: "I'd like to talk with you, as I am unhappy with the results I've been achieving with our sales team and could use your insights." This humility will cause people who may have judged you poorly to give you some space and a chance to show improvement.

My first instructions need a caveat. I don't recommend managing by consensus and, second, I almost always err on the side of being overly kind to the employee. People respond better (in the long term) when you come from a place of kindness rather than of intimidation. However, my first recommendation for you when you take over a new team will seem contrary to this advice.

Your first mission is to decide which person on your team you will fire and to do it within 45 days. Have I made you uncomfortable yet? Give the person a generous severance package and do it with authenticity and as much kindness as possible, but do it. You will use the first 30 days to decide who this will be as you learn about the team. A team learns a lot about what your values are by who is rewarded, promoted, or let go.

Let me explain the why and the how of making this decision. The instinct of a new manager is typically to build consensus, conjure team spirit, and have people be thankful that a new person is in charge: "It's about time!" This instinct will almost always slow down your progress in getting results from your new team. You must remember that you were hired to get results. The best position is to have your new team be "cautiously optimistic." They are hopeful that you'll add real value and fix the things that are wrong, but as of now they haven't decided whether they like or even respect you.

During this first 30-day period, you will be posting an advertisement for a new salesperson. You will be meeting with every person on your sales team, the head of each department in the company, and administrative support staff as well as some customers. You will also be delving deeply into the metrics of the company. We'll discuss the order and content of these meetings and actions. You will end this 30-day period by firing someone on your team and implementing some new Sacred Rhythms.

"But wait," you might say, "what if nobody deserves to be fired?" In my years of working with sales teams, I can count on one hand the number of times that there isn't someone on the sales team who isn't performing or someone who is performing, but has a caustic and unhelpful attitude that hurts the rest of the team. The person fired may be upset for a moment, but it's likely he's unhappy in the role already and will be much more content in a role that is a better fit elsewhere. Your team might be the exception, but I doubt it. Why are you leading this team? My guess is to improve it substantially, not incrementally. So ask yourself: "When this team is performing at the highest level I'll be able to bring them to, who won't be capable of making it?"

You must do this from a place of authenticity, humility, and a sincere desire to improve the team. This is not a power play or a show of authority. It is an appropriate and judicious use of power with a purpose. It is a very effective way to reset the standards for the team and show the seriousness of the situation and need for increasing sales. You will be doing many things in the first 30 days with the mindset of a learner and gaining consensus from the group. Balancing this with decisive action will cause the group to see you as fair and inclusive, but also decisive and action-oriented. It will underscore the fact that change will be happening. Having your team understand that you are fair but decisive is the most effective way to accomplish what you'll need to do in the next six months.

I am always unhappy when someone needs to be fired from a sales team. I believe a company must take it seriously to find the right fit when they are in the hiring process and then coach and mentor that person to success. Anything else is a failure of management. I make an exception in the first 30 days. Someone must go. I know I'll get some disagreement on this point. However, I can tell you from experience and observation that the fastest route to a high-performance culture includes this unpleasant choice.

The first 30 days are like a new theater act playing on Broadway. You walk onto the stage, and your performance in the first act influences the remainder of your time in the role as sales manager. Plan and execute this 30 days with skill. You don't want a poor review from the critics. I'll suggest some key ingredients and the preferred order here, but you will need to adjust them to fit your situation. Please notice I did not say, "Adjust them until you are comfortable." You should be uncomfortable.

## Getting Started with Your Team: The First 30 Days

Day one after the announcement of your role is shared with the team, you must find a simple way to acknowledge your appointment into the role as Sales Boss. This acknowledgment can be through a short email, a company meeting, a video call, or any method that reaches the entire team. The key points of your message:

> "I am humbled to be chosen for this important role and to work with a talented team of people."
>
> "Although I have enjoyed successes in the past, I realize that there is much I need to learn from you. I will be spending the next weeks meeting with folks and learning. After this, I will have more specifics to share with the team and will be hosting a company meeting [give the date]."
>
> "You can expect that I will build on the work that has been accomplished before me, and I will be focused on increasing our success in the marketplace."
>
> "I take success seriously, as I know that none of us can do the things that are important such as buying homes, educating our kids, taking vacations, or retiring without our company being a leader in sales."
>
> "I will be posting an open sales position today and ask anyone who knows of qualified candidates to encourage them to apply."

You will, of course, infuse this short communication with your style and personality, but I believe the messages above should be communicated clearly and passionately. If you are doing this via email (not my first option), you might consider including a link to a humorous YouTube video or something that will humanize you to those who have yet to get to know you. You don't want to be "the corporate guy." Be human, be authentic, and be direct. Schedule an all-company or all-division meeting about five weeks away when you will unveil your thoughts and plan of action.

Next, using Chapter 7 and the information regarding posting an open sales job, you post the salesperson opening and start the search process. Finding and hiring a superstar takes time, and from now on throughout the remainder of your career as Sales Boss, you'll *always keep an open pipeline drawing in qualified candidates, even when you don't currently have an open position.* You never want to be in the position of needing someone and having a lengthy delay in placing a great person in the role. You'll likely have an opening at the end of this month anyhow if you are following my advice.

While you are in this 30-day discovery period, the weekly mechanics of running the sales team still must happen. I suggest keeping existing sales meetings that are already on the schedule. Nothing changes. Simply assign a variety of people on your sales team to lead these meetings and then attend as an observer. This method will keep the existing structures in place, but will also give you a chance to observe the skill level of some of the members of your team. I would announce this with a simple: "We need to keep things rolling while I wrap my head around things here, so I'll ask you guys to take the lead in the meetings for the first month. Who wants to volunteer for the first one?"

Now that this is out of the way, you will need to do a deep dive into the inner workings of the company and your sales team. You will not limit yourself to the people you directly manage. You will also meet with, at a minimum, all of the department heads. Your discovery of the company should take two parts: meeting with people and analyzing data. My suggestion is that your daytime hours be used exclusively for meeting with people and you reserve some late evening/early morning hours for data analysis. You need to know the numbers and data, but you won't want yourself labeled as a data-head in the first few weeks. Relationships will prove to be more valuable than any amount of data.

A key part of success in this period is not to have your boss tell you what he or she thinks of all the people on your sales team before you've had a chance to form your own judgments. If you meet with the boss first, his or her impressions will undoubtedly influence your thoughts and you may waste some time seeking to validate those impressions rather than seeking the truth.

One of the best ways to start learning about the people and processes of the company is to meet with the administrative and support staff before you meet to talk deeply with your boss, peers, or department heads. That's right, start with the people who answer the phones and keep the company running operationally. They know where all the bodies are hidden! The administrative staff will have a surprisingly unvarnished view of the company and, while it usually isn't 100 percent accurate, in my experience, you can bet that the emotional spirit and energy of the company can be detected right away by their observations. They are usually more than ready to share their insights, and nobody has ever asked them. To be fair, they have a higher than 80 percent accuracy, in my experience.

On one consulting assignment, my client asked me to help diagnose some of the sales issues keeping the company from delivering high-quality products and services to their customers. The client sold through numerous distribution channels and also had its independent field sales team. One of the areas of concern was that each of the sales channels was cannibalizing some of the sales of the other channels. I asked them not to tell me what the full issues were, but to give me a couple of weeks to observe the teams and ask them some questions. I shared that I would come back in a few weeks to discuss what direction our project might take together.

Guess where I went first? The lobby. I had earlier in the week eaten lunch at a restaurant recommended to me by the woman who was answering the phone and greeting visitors in the lobby. During our conversations previously, she'd told me they had her favorite banana cream pie. Of course, I brought her a slice when I came back to the company's lobby after eating lunch, and she was grateful. She didn't often get a break away from the phones. Quick tip: Always be nice to the support staff, as they can grease the wheels to speed your progress or bring you to a screeching halt!

This time, I asked her whether she could chat for a bit "off the record." She was only too pleased. She gave me a quick rundown of who was who and who had the power regardless of what the titles might indicate. She suggested some other support people I could talk with who would have some great insights. I spent the next week and a half touring around and talking with all the people she had suggested. As I pulled on the "string" she had handed me, it would lead me to numerous discoveries that would prove helpful later in my diagnosis and potential remedy.

A few weeks passed, and it was time to meet again with the executive team. I laid out for them some of the things that I had learned, while protecting the information shared with me in confidence. I was able to articulate many of the problems between departments that were causing the issues and challenges the executive team had concerns about. I was also in the position of sketching out the beginning of a plan to improve these areas. About midway through my presentation, one of the executives said with astonishment: "It seems like you've been inside our company forever! How did you learn so much in this short a time? I've been here three years and didn't know some of this." He had just paid me a large consulting fee. Do you think he wanted to hear that I took his secretaries to lunch and asked them? I told him anyway. It was a lesson worth learning, and you should also learn it. Talk to the support staff before talking to the executive team. If you do this in reverse order, your insights won't be as clear because you will have absorbed the bias of the executive team. You will talk to the executive team, and their insights will be equally as valuable, but I think the order here is important to avoid weighted biases. It is worth mentioning that one of the things we helped implement for the company saved them $10 million per year in annual expenses. This idea came directly from a secretary.

So what should these discovery conversations cover? I'll give you a short list of the types of questions for each type of person you are meeting with, just to get you started. Give some thought to your specific company and add to this list of questions. They will be general in nature. It is important that you bring your full EQ to these meetings and guard against any pontification on your thoughts and ideas. These must be learning sessions. Bring your curious self, not your teaching self or your ego.

Questions for support staff might include:

- How long have you worked here?
- What other departments have you been in and what roles have you had here?
- What areas do you think are most important about the work your department does?
- What ends up being the most frustrating thing?
- How long has that been a problem?
- What have you [your department] tried to do to fix it?
- Did that work?
- Where did you work previously?
- What did they do better than we do?
- What do we do better?
- What does your group think about my sales team?
- Do they deserve that view in your opinion?
- I'm curious. Do you know [name of the salesperson]?

- What has been your experience with him or her?
- What is his or her personality?
- How often does he or she interact with your group?
- If you were in charge of my sales team and could change something, what would you change?

I hope that this list helps you start thinking of some additional questions you'll ask. You might find that some will be bashful and give you a noncommittal answer such as "I'm not sure." Remember that people may not have been asked their opinions and they haven't learned to trust you yet. I find that in those cases if you'll gently prod them with humor and a smile and say something like "That's OK if you had to guess—I'm not holding you to it!" They'll usually relent and give you their opinions.

The questions for the department heads will be very similar and include the ones above; however, I would also include questions such as:

- When you started here, what was the first thing you saw that you needed to change?
- How did that go?
- How did you approach it?
- What was people's reaction?
- What is the most important issue facing your team now?
- What do you think I'll need to do to be successful in my role?
- Are there any unwritten rules I should be aware of at the company?
- Tell me about the people who have been in my role previously.
- If you could replicate one of my team members, who would it be? Why?

- Is there anyone on my team you think won't make it or is hurting the company? Why?
- When I need help from your group, what's the best way to approach receiving that help?

When meeting with department heads, you will also have asked them to give you presentations or overviews of their groups as they relate to sales. So the marketing team would give you an overview of the marketing strategy, advertising spend, and so forth.

Continue to set up meetings and ask these types of questions and listen to their presentations until you've interviewed all of the key department heads and the key support staff. You will find that a common theme will emerge and you will have a good insight into the state of affairs as it is today. Be cautious that you do not accept everything you hear as true, but simply honor the knowledge as the sincere viewpoint of the person who shared it with you. You must do the work of deciding over time whether that view is accurate and helpful to your goal of building a successful sales team. I would also caution you to treat these conversations as confidential and "off the record."

You will observe that I have suggested some meetings, and that these also come before you spend much time with your team. You will be interacting with your team during this period, but the deep questions with them will usually come nearer to week three than week one. This time gap allows you to gain a sense of things before you become attached to people on your team. It is always true that you will naturally like some members of your team better than others and that this propensity will cause you to judge things differently. I don't think we can ever eliminate this entirely, but we must be on guard against it. Some of the best members of my sales team have sometimes been people I didn't want a social relationship with or didn't connect with on the deepest level. We were different personalities, but both of us were very capable at our jobs. Be careful that you don't dismiss a person's excellence just because he doesn't perform in your preferred style. Start intermixing deeper, more focused conversations with your individual salespeople as you near the end of week two and enter week three. Avoid giving your thoughts and opinions. You must remain in learning mode. When people finally learn your thoughts about matters, you'll want to share them in a controlled and planned way, which we will discuss shortly.

It must also be your goal during these initial weeks to meet face-to-face with some of your customers. When you have these customer meetings, include people from your sales team. I would suggest no fewer than ten customer visits. While you are making customer visits, also ride along on a prospecting call with a salesperson when possible. Let the salesperson run these meetings so that you get the double benefit of meeting the customer while observing the style and approach of your salesperson. Try to do these visits with a good sampling of the sales team. Depending on the size of your team, you may be able to include a customer visit alongside each of your team members, which would be ideal. Don't give coaching on these visits; just focus on the customer and learn a bit about the salesperson. After all, will it serve you better for your salesperson to tell you how he does it or for you to actually see how? When you are in the field traveling with your sales team, turn off your phone. Agree on set break times that you both will use to catch up on emails and phone calls, but model uninterrupted attention.

I use Evernote to keep organized with all of these interviews and other meetings. Evernote is an amazing tool that allows you to organize your life. Not only can you take notes, but you can also attach websites, files, audio recordings, pictures, or just about anything else right into Evernote. The magic (and it does seem like magic) is in how you can later access the data. When I take a note, it stamps the note with the location I am in or guesses based on my calendar what this note might be related to. When I return to a physical location it pulls all of the notes from the last time I was at the location and makes them readily available. I can record conversations from within Evernote. I could go on and on, but just suffice it to say that if you don't have a good system, then you should try Evernote. And if you are "old school" and still like paper and pen, you can still do that and have it show up as a searchable document in Evernote. This is super helpful if, when reflecting on the meetings you have held, you want to find the person who shared such-and-such with you.

Let's turn our attention to the data analytics. If the company has a great CRM system, you will want to run some reports that will help you. My experience is that poorly run teams tend to have sloppy data. You'll soon discover what the case is with your company. Here are some key data points that I think are imperative to look at:

- How many salespeople has the company hired in the last five years?
- How many has the company fired overall?
- What is the average length of employment for a salesperson?
- What are the average sales of a new salesperson historically at years one through five?
- What is the average yearly per person sales average for the sales team?
- What is the average for the top performer?
- What is the average for the bottom performer?
- How long does it currently take to train a new salesperson to full capacity?
- What is the current hiring process?

- How long does it historically take to hire someone?
- How long does it typically take the company to fire someone who doesn't perform?
- How many new customers is the sale team bringing on each year?
- What percentage of sales is to repeat customers?
- What is the average sales total of an order by niche?
- What are the current steps in the sales process?
- Are the steps clearly defined?
- How long is the sales process from start to sale?
- What is the size of the sales prospect universe?
- What percentage of the industry do we represent?
- What is our total proposal volume?
- What is the proposal process?
- How long does it take to turn around a quote?
- What is our win/loss percentage?
- If we travel as a sales team, what percentage of time is spent traveling?
- How does the amount of time traveling compare among team members?
- Is there a travel time/sales success connection?
- What types of prospecting are done by the team?
- What percentage of time do individual salespeople spend prospecting?
- What training collaterals are available?
- What sales collateral is available?
- What is the web traffic?
- What is the conversion rate on web leads?
- How many leads does the team receive?
- When we win, why do we win?
- When we lose, why do we lose?
- What is our sales overhead per new sale?
- What are our customer service scores?

- What are our delivery times?
- How well does our CRM support the needs of sales?
- What regular meetings does the team hold?
- What ongoing training has been provided by the company in the past?
- What is the current compensation plan?
- Is the current compensation plan effective?
- When was the compensation plan last changed?
- What impact did the change have?
- How well was this change in compensation received by the team?
- What is the current sales forecast?
- Where are sales in comparison to the budget?
- How was the forecast prepared?
- How likely are we to achieve forecast?

This list is just a start. You should become a serious student of each area of the sales team. You must commit to learning as much as possible and as fast as possible. In the upcoming months, your knowledge and insights will undoubtedly deepen, but you must become functionally literate in the things affecting your sales team and the results they achieve so that you can start implementing a plan, even if it is not yet perfect. You should have a working knowledge in the first three to four weeks. This may seem like a huge task, so I will share with you what my mentor would say to me whenever he gave me a bunch of things to accomplish in a short period. He was fond of saying, "I know you can't get all of this accomplished today, so feel free to work all night!"

Next, take a working vacation. As you come to the end of your third or fourth week since becoming the sales manager, schedule yourself for a three-day vacation. I'm not talking about a vacation away on a tropical island. I have a working vacation in

Sketch the outline of your plan:

- Who will be fired?
- Who might be fired?
- Who needs retraining?
- What critical areas must be focused on?
- Who is our enemy?
- Who are our heroes?
- What are we the best at?
- Who is your best player?
- Is this person the absolute best in our industry or just *our best*?
- How do we win?
- What systems should be in place to support a win?
- What Sacred Rhythms should you implement for your team?
- What rituals does your team have?
- What language will help them increase the sense of belonging?

That's a lot of work. Take a nap. How do you feel after sleeping on it? Make whatever changes you need to make to your plan.

## Day two

Run your plan past a few people. Doing this will give you practice in how to articulate the plan in a clear way; will allow you to hear the types of questions, thoughts, and objections your plan may face; and will allow you to gain some early feedback. Approach people one-to-one so they have the ability to give you their unique insights and so you avoid group-think. Because you will be working off-site, use Skype or some other videoconferencing tool to hold these discussions. Using video allows you to observe people's reactions, as well as listening to what they say. Here are the specific people I suggest you talk with today:

- Your boss or "The" Boss, the person whose support you'll need if you plan to implement the plan
- An outside mentor with experience, perhaps a seasoned Sales Boss from another company
- Another key department head within the company whose support would influence others in the company
- The person on your sales team with the most unofficial influence on the other team members

Working your way through this list and the conversations you have will provide you with very valuable insights. It also will serve the purpose of market testing your ideas, since you know that what you discuss with them won't likely stay confidential. The salesperson you talk to will leak a bit of your plan to the rest of the team. This type of sharing has the advantage of letting them get used to the ideas before their formal introduction. If there is an extreme reaction, you'll likely hear it before you make the plan formal. In fact, many times you'll get these early warnings directly from the support staff that you spent so much time talking to at the outset. They'll be rooting for you to have success and will point out a few landmines as they see them. This reaction doesn't necessarily mean you'll change your plan (although you might); it simply will help you understand what areas you will need to sell better than others.

By the evening of the second day, you'll have plenty of things to reflect on. Make some final adjustments to your plan.

## Day three

You should spend today planning the content of the meeting you will hold with the company outlining your plan and course of action. You may not share every detail, but you will want to think about how and what you can share. When people hear your presentation, they should understand how you arrived at your decisions and should even feel that these decisions are the obvious conclusions. They should be clear about the impact of the changes, the direction you plan to go, and why. They should know the name of the enemy and what "greatest" means. They should know the consequence of failure to the future of the company. This presentation should leave them feeling inspired and trusting your process for making a decision, even if they don't agree with what you've decided. If you intermix some of the stories you heard from them when you met with them individually, then you will be telling them their story and they'll connect with it emotionally to support you because you listened.

This presentation needs emotion, emotion, and more emotion. Passion must also play a role in the way you design the presentation. You must tell a story full of emotion. Where we are today. Where we need to be. How we will get there. Introduce a few of the new Sacred Rhythms and rituals that your team will live by in the upcoming months. Tell them why you believe in rituals, perhaps sharing a family ritual you cherished when growing up. Sharing these personal details will humanize you and create the start of intimacy with your team.

Data should be present, but only to highlight the story. Pick some bold visuals to represent ideas, not PowerPoint bullets. If the story is: "Our house is on fire and we need major change!" the data can show the precipitous drop in market share and the jobs that the company will be losing if the trend is unchanged. If the story is: "We've been the leader, but now we are at a plateau," the data can show that story, but then you must give examples of companies that failed to break out of the plateau and others that were successful.

Do this as an exercise: Write a one-paragraph summary of your story and give the story a one-sentence title. Is it compelling? If not, start over. This story will serve as the foundation for all the changes you'll be making with the team.

Now you should choose someone with whom to share the story you've created. Is the person compelled or bored after hearing it? Work today to get the story right. Plan how you will share this at your first meeting with the full group and how you'll reinforce it in upcoming months.

Write your 90-day to-do list. Know that it will change, so continue to be flexible.

Finally, who do you plan to fire?

Nobody? I'm fine with that choice if you arrived at it after a vigorous search and real consideration of the option. You have a problem though if you are choosing not to take this step because you are uncomfortable or believe that everyone deserves a second chance.

More likely, you will have a name or perhaps even a few names of people who won't be a fit for your team. Choose one. You should only let one person go at this point. I have found that a mass firing and the emotional impact on the remaining team that comes with it are too severe to overcome quickly. Usually, when you pick one person, the remaining part of the team—and indeed the company—has known for a long time that the person wasn't a fit. All will be thankful that someone finally acted! If there are others who need to go, wait a bit to assess the impact the first action has on the team.

Meet with the salesperson and let him or her go from employment. There is no need for a long discussion. You are giving a generous severance package and you wish the person well. You have simply decided that the person's skill set doesn't match what you need in the sales position for that territory moving forward. Of course, this book doesn't cover all of the

What is this mythical creature called the superstar salesperson? If you've ever had one on your team, you know the value that such a person adds. They consistently out-perform their peers. They relentlessly slay dragons, bring home the bacon, and make it look easy. They live to sell. This chapter is designed to help you get them on your team. Once you have one, make sure you take good care of him or her. These people will make everything else you and the company need to do easier.

## Why Hiring a Superstar Salesperson Is Tough

Perhaps nothing is more difficult and more important for the success of a business than hiring the right salespeople. Remember, in any business nothing happens until somebody sells something! Nobody pays the mortgage, no kids are sent to college, no retirements are funded until the salespeople can close business and bring revenue in the door. Unfortunately for many companies, hiring a salesperson has become a bit like buying a boat, the happiest day being when one is bought (hired) and the second happiest being the day it is sold (fired).

Just consider your experience. You decide the time is right to add a salesperson to the team and you excitedly begin tallying up how an "X" increase in the business will solve so many of the challenges facing your company. You know that additional customers and revenue will create the exact thing your company needs right now to achieve its goals. You post the job, you sort through résumés, you spend time interviewing, and eventually you have what you believe to be the perfect candidate. You make a job offer. What happens next?

For many companies the honeymoon period starts, but it wears off quickly! The dreams we had of increased sales languish, and we wonder what went wrong. We start to question our decision. We think: "Maybe just a little more coaching or more time and then she'll start to perform?" Eventually, you start to regret the decision, and as you shell out paycheck after paycheck to a mediocre salesperson, you start to resent the person. Eventually, you fire her or she quits. And now the process starts again, only this time you are a bit more jaded.

If this sounds familiar, pay particular attention to this section. We'll identify some common pitfalls that occur in the hiring process. We'll also talk a bit about what things could be going on that are hurting your chance to add a sales superstar to your team. Let's be clear: Superstars do exist. Let's commit to hiring them.

Great salespeople are always in demand. The problem is that there are so few of them. Even in a tough economy, a company will rarely ever let go of a salesperson who is consistent in generating revenue. The reason is somewhat obvious, right? When times are tough, a company will downsize the least productive salespeople. They let go of the ones who could do OK while everyone was buying, but who struggle when they have to earn or influence the buying decision. This reality means that, as the one making the hiring decision, you face a supply-side shortage. You must be able to lure away the top talent from your competition or understand some of the market forces that are in play that allow you to nab a superstar who is between jobs. Just understanding that an unemployed salesperson is an automatic red flag will improve your odds of success. Notice I didn't say, "No great salesperson will be unemployed." I simply said, "It's a red flag." Your process must be designed to get to the truth of why someone is unemployed.

Understand the psychology of the situation. Put yourself on the other side of the equation. Let's say you are the superstar salesperson. What's your life like right now? Pretty good, I'd imagine! At your company, it's likely that you are viewed as a hero. You are pulling in some good cash, winning awards and travel vacations because of your super performance. Chances are, you can do pretty much what you want as long as you keep delivering those stellar sales numbers. You've probably built up some repeat business, you have your routine down, and you know just which levers to pull to get things done for your customers. Do you see my point? Why am I, "superstar," switching jobs? I'm usually not.

Even when tempted by another great-looking position at some other company, a superstar considers things pretty carefully. We've all heard the phrase "Better the devil I know than the one I don't!" This saying is certainly true when a salesperson has succeeded in selling for a company. So beware of the unemployed.

Even mediocre salespeople are A-players when it comes to selling themselves. They've been to enough sales training that they'll be able to talk prospecting, pipelines, sales ratios, and closing techniques. They just won't be able to do those things at a superstar level. The good news is that selling is a very metrics-driven process, and a good hiring process will uncover the truth.

If you are hiring someone who is unemployed, you must understand the reason. Possible reasons that a superstar is unemployed or looking elsewhere include:

- The current company just went through a merger or buyout. (Carefully watching the industry news can help you identify potential sales candidates.)
- Relocation requirements.
- A new sales manager has been put in place, and a conflict exists. (Be suspect on this one.)

- Significant market changes that the salesperson's company has not kept pace with has decreased sales opportunities. (Lack of product innovation as an example.)
- The company has significantly changed or capped the person's earning potential.

There are more reasons that I haven't listed, but I hope you can see the common thread here. Something has changed that is outside the control of the salesperson that he or she is not in a position to influence or change. The person simply wants to make money. The person has done the calculus; the rules and opportunities have changed, so he or she is looking elsewhere.

Don't believe the simple statement: "I'm just looking for a more challenging assignment." Rarely is this true. I'd almost go so far as to say *never*. A good hiring process will uncover and get to this vital truth. We'll discuss the specifics later in this book.

Before we go into the specifics of making the hiring decision and the process, let's discuss one other important aspect: you and your company. Maybe you have managed to hire a superstar, but you've blown it in the execution. Think this is impossible? Think again. Make certain that you have created the right sales conditions for success.

As an example, imagine you go to the plant nursery and purchase a beautiful plant that looks healthy and vibrant. You take that plant home, plant it in a pot on your porch, and within weeks it starts to shrivel. Is the only plausible explanation that you've purchased a bad plant? Not likely! You may have planted it in the wrong soil, placed it in too much sunshine, failed to feed it correctly, or a host of other issues. At least be open to the fact that when a salesperson fails, it can be your fault.

You must be the kind of company that can support a superstar, and you have to be honest about the selling environment you are asking that person to sell in. Does your marketing team provide plenty of well-qualified leads? If not, be honest and hire the salesperson who is great at generating his or her own leads. Will your new salesperson have to service the accounts he's sold in addition to having made the sale? It is your job to do an honest evaluation of your selling process (or lack thereof) and be certain that the person you are hiring has done well in a similar environment. If he hasn't made a cold call in years, he'll struggle if that's what you require for success in your company. This concept is true no matter how talented the person is in other areas of selling.

Focus on the selling environments that the person was successful in previously. Great Sales Success + Mediocre Environment = Great Salesperson. On the other hand, if the environment was Great Sales Success + Great Selling Environment, it could = mediocre salesperson if *your* selling environment isn't as great as the environment of the company the person is coming from. The key here is: Great selling results don't always mean a great salesperson. It only means that sometimes. It could also mean the person was in a great company that was a leader in its niche. The person could have been working for the lowest cost option or any other host of variables that made him or her have some measure of selling success. It's your job to uncover the truth through your hiring process.

# Step by Step to Hiring a Sales Superstar

# The Selection Process

Running a great selection process requires the right mindset and proper preparation. The enemy of great is the rushed process: "I just needed someone yesterday!"

I'd like you to imagine that you were getting ready to invest a half-million dollars of your company's money, or better yet, think of investing your own money. How carefully would you consider the investment? In most cases more money, expense, and revenue hinge on making a good hiring decision for a sales position than just half a million. Treat the decision with the importance it deserves. Here are the critical steps in the process of hiring a sales superstar.

## Design a well-written job posting

Take the time to identify what skills are required to be successful. Describe these skills clearly in the advertisement, rather than just describing the industry or product they'll be asked to sell.

- What type of prospecting will they do?
- What type of record-keeping will they use?
- What support structure will they have?
- Is it a complex sell?
- Will they be selling once to an individual?
- Is it a multi-call sales process?
- Will they be presenting to larger groups?
- Is it an RFP process?

- Are you the highest priced solution?
- Are you the lowest cost solution?
- How intense is the competition?
- Where do you rank in size and quality to your competition?
- Are salespeople expected to find new clients and pass them on to customer care?
- Will they sell and service the clients?

You should be asking and answering all of these types of questions as you create the job posting. Your goal is for salespeople to see how their own past successes match up to your requirements and self-select out of the process if they don't think they have what it takes.

The job posting should include a realistic earning figure and expectation. When I say "expectation," I don't mean they could expect to earn this much. I mean, *you* expect them to earn that much or they'll not be working for your company. There is a big difference in the way you convey that number. Superstars don't want or need blue-sky numbers. They want real earning expectations.

You might word the portion dealing with compensation this way: "A successful candidate will have a history of making $90,000 per year, of which 30 percent should have been variable compensation, and a need to make $125,000."

Once you've decided someone might be the right person to hire, you should always verify the person's earnings claim by asking for a past W-2 form or whatever form is available in your country that will help verify income. Candidates have done what they claimed they have or they haven't. When do you want to find out? After you've hired someone or before? Try this to encourage honesty: "If we decide that you would be a fit for our sales position and you decide you'd like to accept the role, we'll be asking you to verify your past earnings through your W-2."

My experience has been that this results in more honest answers right from the start!

Describe your industry, but don't limit the industries that you'll accept. You might say: "Experience selling to [your industry segment] helpful but not required." It is more important that the daily selling activities you will require of them have been a part of their recent experience and success than specific industry experience. Obviously, if you can get both, that's ideal. *But never give industry preference over activity successes.* As an example, one of my clients in the food processing industry needed someone who could cold-call new prospects consistently. They could have limited themselves to salespeople who had previous experience in the food processing industry. Instead, they focused on the need to make cold calls. They ended up hiring someone with no industry experience, but who had made cold calls every day in the recruiting industry. That hire ended up outperforming any previous sales hire.

Remember to hire primarily for previous relevant types of sales activity and not primarily industry experience. Don't limit the candidates who will apply by arbitrarily adding qualifications that aren't an absolute necessity. For instance, many companies will state that they require a college degree. Ask yourself: "If this person is a superstar and can sell in our environment to our clients, do I care if he has the degree?" If the answer is "No, I don't," then don't include it in the posting. Some of the best businesspeople and salespeople haven't been to college. That is why many times they are in sales and out-earning the college grad with the MBA. They knew if they wanted to earn a healthy paycheck, they had better learn to sell.

Finally, you will also want to include in the job posting a request such as: "Please provide in your cover letter an example of a recent selling success you've had that demonstrates your suitability for the role." This request serves two purposes. One, in the age of online applications, you will get hundreds of applicants who are mass applying for anything with the term sales in the job title. By adding this tiny request, you will know they've read your posting. Second, it gives you an insight into how they approach sales and how they communicate. Here is a recent job posting created for a client [edited to protect company name]:

Sample Company is seeking to add two salespeople to their team. One will be based in the Mid-Atlantic and another in a Southeast territory. Ideally, the successful candidates will be in place prior to the start of _____. Our hiring process is thorough, but moves quickly for the right candidate.

Mid-Atlantic: VA, WV, KY, NC, SC
Southeast: GA, FL, AL, MS, TN

**About You**

You are an accomplished salesperson with the ability to work from a home office located within your assigned territory and travel to visit customers and prospects 60 to 70 percent of the month. You have an ability to prospect consistently on the phone, in person, and at company trade events. Knowledge of the packaging industry, primarily in food, meats, medical, and bakery markets, is preferred, but not required if you have a history of sales success in a complex selling environment, the ability to learn quickly, and can retain knowledge. You are adept at selling solutions that exceed $200,000 to upwards of $1M. You are well spoken, can command a room's attention, and have high energy levels. People consider you a leader and you consider a sales territory as your personal business. You are accustomed to tracking your sales behavior and metrics as a source of effectiveness and improvement. While already operating at a high level, you understand and accept training and coaching as a source of constant growth.

You must have a verifiable history of earning in excess of $90,000 and a need to quickly surpass $150,000. Our top earners in the field regularly surpass $200,000 in yearly earnings excluding company benefits. Salespeople who fail to earn at a high level are not kept at Sample Company, as our reputation, line of equipment, and sales leads provide ample opportunity for selling.

Please include in your application a cover letter with the answer to these questions: What do you consider the key to sales success? and What is one of your greatest selling successes to date? Applications without this information in the cover letter will not be considered. Feel like this job is perfect for you but you don't fit one of the criteria? Sell us on why you should be hired anyway.

**About Sample Company**

Sample Company is a leader in complete packaging solutions to the food, medical device, personal care, and industrial industries. For over 15 years, Sample Company has worked closely with our customers to engineer superior intelligent primary and secondary solutions. Our goal is to make our customers more competitive by becoming more efficient. Our installed base speaks for itself. We will not shy away from a project due to complexity; rather we address

*(Continued)*

*(Continued)*

each component head on. Our access to global solutions makes Sample Company a forerunner in packaging technologies today. Sample Company offers a competitive salary, 401K and benefits package, and full headquarters support.

Did you notice the focus on the *type of person* rather than specifics of the company position? This type of ad stands out among the clutter on hiring websites and serves as a magnet for top performers. Here is an actual portion of a cover letter submitted by an applicant in response to the posting:

"Just reading the way the job roles were 'pitched' has created a high level of interest in Sample Company. I have a solid history of selling systems and consumables to national and international customers. Having studied the company website also, I am convinced it would be worthwhile to meet the hiring manager to communicate how my abilities and sales skill set would benefit Sample Company. I like that the job pitch was not a long job description, but rather lays down a challenge to prospective sales employees that success is rewarded, but failure is not supported. I really like the way this was described, having confidence to exceed goals within a direct and pragmatic company culture. One example of selling success I can give is . . ."

Now that you have a solid job posting, go post the job. I won't cover the many job sites available, as it'd be out-of-date as soon as I wrote it and effectiveness varies by industry and geography. Your network should be able to recommend some solid places to post. Don't neglect the trade journals and websites of your industry, along with the same sites for parallel industries, meaning industries that have a very similar selling process (not the product) as you have in your company.

In addition to posting the job, you should email the posting to as many people in your network as possible with a brief note asking them whether they know anyone who fits what you have described. A word of caution is in order here. If someone in your network recommends a salesperson to you, it is very easy to allow how you feel about the person making the referral influence how you rate the candidate. Sometimes I see companies shortcut their hiring process when dealing with someone referred to them. They almost always regret it. No matter the source of the candidate, always follow your process. Remember that your contact has likely referred the person because he or she likes the person or wants to be of help to you. People usually haven't made the suggestion because they have any knowledge of how well the person will do in your company selling your product to your customers.

Now that you've posted the job, you should also proactively reach out to targeted people at other companies whom you may want to consider for the position. Remember that the very best salespeople aren't usually in the market, so you'll have to lure them to take a look at your opportunity. If you want to increase your odds of successfully luring someone, you can go back and read the list of reasons why a superstar might be changing jobs and target those companies. For instance, has there been a recent merger in your industry? If so, it's likely that at least a few top performers are unhappy with the changes at the new company and might be open to a job change. The trade journals are a good source for this type of target.

Spend some time on LinkedIn reaching out to potential targets. If you pay for the recruiter version or any of the premium memberships, you'll have advanced search features that can help you identify potential salespeople. In fact, you can even search by past companies that they've worked for if you know a company's reputation for producing great salespeople. Be creative and find people to place in your process. Tip: LinkedIn limits your view of people to three degrees, so it's very helpful to expand your searchable network by joining groups or paying for the recruiter's version.

An important note here is that you will want to keep the process moving. Don't wait until all the candidates have applied before you take the next step. Think of the entire process as a river that is constantly flowing bringing you candidates. When I say "next do this," it simply means do this next with the pool of candidates who are at a particular stage in the process. Superstar candidates never stay on the market for long.

Eventually, you will want to work on creating such a strong brand for your company that the best candidates seek you out. This likely isn't the position you are in when you take over as the Sales Boss, but it is something you should take ownership of now that you are in charge of the team. All great programmers at least consider an interview request from Apple or Google, and in the same way, you want to become the company that great salespeople take the call from. Some simple steps in this regard can be including some great videos about your company on your hiring website as well as focusing on the feel and tone of your social media presence online. Now for the next step.

## Dissect the résumé

Now that you have a list of applicants and a stack of résumés, you will need to decide which ones to connect with. This is mind-numbingly dull work! I don't care whether you are using an electronic applicant tracking system (ATS) or you just have paper stacks of résumés; this is an ugly process. Buckle down and get it done. Move quickly, as the best candidates will not be available for long. You don't have the luxury of taking a long time for the process. If you do, you'll lose the best and be stuck with mediocre.

I suggest the three-pile method:

1. Not a chance
2. Maybe
3. Worth a look

If you followed my earlier advice and asked that the candidates write custom responses to a question, you can start by placing the non-compliant ones in stacks number 1 or 2 if you have enough candidates.

Don't be fooled (sold) by fancy visuals and creative writing. Remember that many résumés are solid works of fiction, and most of them have been embellished creatively. Sometimes the worst looking résumé is the superstar, as it has been a long time since the person has applied for a new job. It never occurs to the superstar that he'll be judged by anything other than proven performance. The best looking résumé is often the result of someone with lots of job-seeking experience. I'm guessing that is not exactly the kind of experience you were looking for when you started the search. Primarily you should be looking for evidence that the person has had success in the same type of selling environment that exists at your company. Think back to the list of questions in the section on creating the job posting. How many does the candidate match? The more, the better!

Make certain that they clearly articulate that they are looking for a sales job, not a sales management job or a marketing/

sales job. Don't hire the long-term sales manager who wants back into sales. You want to hire the salesperson who has been out demonstrating the selling skills that you will consistently need.

What about the length of employment at previous jobs? In today's environment, the reality is that people change jobs more frequently than in the past. Count the number of years at each role and write it in the margins. My guess is you'll see a pattern. The person switches jobs every three years, or whatever. This should not automatically disqualify that person, but you should understand that if he of she works for you, you would have the person for a similar length of time. Will the time and energy and the length of your sales process make this person worthwhile to consider? With all else being equal, your best salespeople don't change positions frequently.

One pattern you will see with some great salespeople is one lengthy period of employment followed by two or three quick job changes. I'm not bothered by this pattern, as it sometimes means they did very well selling at a company; something changed, and now they've been actively looking. They've taken a few roles only to discover quickly that the job wasn't what they thought it'd be. You'll discover the facts during your interview process. One pattern that disturbs me based on my experiences is when someone has been in a selling role then tried to start his or her own business and failed so now is returning to the perceived safety of a sales job.

As you read the résumés, underline any phrases that articulate some result, such as: "Increased sales by x percent" or "Was the number two producer." You will use these statements later in the interview process. How many résumés made it to pile 3?

Let's discuss the interviews. Every company will have a slightly different process, so I will simply outline an effective process for most companies. If you choose to do something different, make sure you understand why the stage was included in my process and the impact of any change you decide to make. For instance, I suggest a phone screening. Some will decide they only have a handful of qualified candidates with the correct set of skills outside of the selling skills needed (for instance, maybe they also need to be a doctor or engineer, or have some very specialized knowledge), so they'll choose to skip this step. This might make sense.

## The Four-Stage Interview Process

This is an area people get wrong. They get it wrong because most of us have a healthy desire to be liked by others. What happens is that they begin the process of interviewing and play the role of "nice guy/gal." They want the candidate to want to work for the company, so they spend a lot of time making the candidate feel welcomed.

I'm going to suggest that you adopt a new mindset. Your role is to make sure that no sales imposter makes it onto your team. Visualize someone in your company you like and admire. Then imagine that you'll have to lay that person off if you let the wrong person join the sales team. What is the emotion you feel as you tell the person you can no longer afford to pay her? Capture that feeling and bring it to the interview. The reality isn't that far off. If your sales team is filled with bad salespeople, eventually the company closes its doors. This is critical. You must get it right, and your co-workers are counting on you. Also, if you become known as the sales manager who has a revolving door of new hires who don't work out, I can guarantee that one day soon your manager will be showing you the exit. Almost nothing hurts your credibility as a manager as much as a poor hire.

Your focus will be on being polite, but direct. Your role is not to make the candidate comfortable. In fact, the best sales interview keeps the candidate slightly off balance. After all, you'll want to see how people perform under stress since they'll likely be calling on prospects who aren't always eager to see them and have their guard up. To be successful in selling, they'll have mastered the skill of bonding and building rapport. Let them do the work on the interview. You focus on finding the truth.

I'll outline a four-stage interview process. I'll list the stages here and then delve into the specific goals of each:

1. Ten-minute phone screening
2. Pressure interview
3. Performance interview
4. Romance interview

## The ten-minute phone screening

The goal of the phone screening is simple. Do you want to use any time visiting with the person in the next interview? Let's be honest: Sometimes you can tell right away that someone won't fit. I'd prefer to discover that on a phone call rather than in my office. End the call as soon as you know there isn't a fit. Follow a tight script. Again, you should be polite, but not work overly hard to make people comfortable. That's their job.

Here is a script that has been used effectively for thousands of screening calls:

> "Hi [candidate's name], this is [your name and company] calling for your interview. We were scheduled for a quick ten minutes. Does this time still work?"
>
> "Great! We've had a lot of responses to our posting, so I apologize for working quickly today. My goal is to identify the top three people to hold a lengthier in-person interview with our team. We only have one spot open

and want to make sure we find the best person for the role. Fair?"

"What do you know about [Company Name]?" [Regardless of response, simply say "OK" and move on.]

"What in your experience qualifies you for this role as written?"

"How would you describe yourself as a salesperson?"

"Describe your current sales job."

"How do you organize your week?" [Regardless of the answer, simply say in a questioning tone: "And that works?" This may make the person uncomfortable or defensive. Pay attention to the response, as it's how he likely will act with your prospects. Is he confident? Does he use humor? Does he try to put you at ease? Or is he simply defensive?]

"I'd like you to complete my sentence. 'Most salespeople fail because _____.'"

"I have a question about your cover letter." [Ask an appropriate question. This simply lets a candidate know this is a personal interview, not a mass interview.]

"Do you currently prospect for new business? If so, how?"

[If she says "by phone," say, "Great! Let's role play that for a minute. I'm the prospect, and I just picked up the phone and said hello. . . .go!"

[If she says "by networking," adjust the role play. The key is to hear people verbalize what they have been saying in their last sales roles. You should immediately detect whether they are comfortable and proficient. You can certainly discover whether someone hasn't prospected in ages! Someone who has done this will have it down and it will roll off the tongue easily. Play the nice prospect. You aren't trying to trick them here. If they fumble somewhat, just say, "It's fine. Would you like to start over?" You are simply trying to see how at ease they are at something they should have done hundreds of times in their selling careers.]

[Don't give any impression of how you think the person did. Simply state: "How do you think that was? Was that a fair reflection of you?"]

"Describe your best sale from initial contact to close." [Pay attention to how "real" it sounds. Was the candidate involved and leading the sale or just around when it happened? You'll hear the difference! Once he finishes his account, ask: "Why did you pick that example?" The answer here will reveal much about how the person views selling.]

[End the call.] "That's all the time we have. We'll be contacting the top three candidates to schedule in-person interviews. What's the best email to use to schedule that?"

It is important that you rate the responses to each question on a 1- to 3-point scale, with 3 being the best response. Go with your gut on this and don't over-think it. Rate them as they answer. It won't be as effective if you wait until the end of the call to complete your ratings.

Give an additional 3 bonus points if you found yourself "liking" someone at the end of the call. This means, did the person succeed in putting you at ease? Did you enjoy the call? Did you start forgetting it was an interview? If so, it's also likely the person will be good at developing rapport with your company's prospects.

Give 1 additional point for each of the following:

- Did the person have good tone and pacing?
- Was he or she articulate?

- Did the person try to ask you questions during the call, especially when you tried to end the call? A great candidate will try to keep you on the call to learn more specifics about the opportunity.

Tally up the total points and schedule the best for the next interview. Remember to move fast, as the best candidates won't be on the market for long. Can you get them in tomorrow? Would a video call for the next interview finish the process sooner? Make it happen as soon as possible.

The best email invitations help frame some of the expectations for performance. Remember that the salesperson is also judging you. Here is a sample that you could edit and use.

---

[Name],

Thank you for the time we spent on the phone today. We would love to have the opportunity to spend more time getting to know you and understanding whether you would be a fit for our sales team. We pride ourselves on building a great company with happy, successful people.

We have the following dates/times available: [List options or use a scheduling link so they can schedule right on your calendar.]

You can learn more about us here: [website, social accounts, etc.]

To reiterate, we are seeking to hire one candidate to add to our sales team. A successful candidate will be someone with a proven record of sales success who is still willing to work hard perfecting his or her skills. A new hire will be expected

*(Continued)*

(*Continued*)

to travel every other week visiting prospects and customers in a defined territory. Our new candidates are expected to earn a minimum of [insert figure], including base salary and commissions. Failure to achieve this number consistently will result in termination. We maintain this policy because we know salespeople need realistic earning figures when considering employment and we know what is achievable in our territories due to our metrics.

If you decide to accept an interview, please bring with you to the interview any sales collateral that you use in your current position when visiting a prospect, such as brochures, PowerPoint, etc.

Our process also includes a final interview. We expect this process to be completed quickly, by [date].

Let me know what works for you. We look forward to seeing you.

Notice some key points in the email: We expect success and continuous learning. We know our sales process and the results we can expect from a new sales hire. We give an earning expectation and clearly state that this job is based on performance. We also outline the remaining stages in the process and give a date for finishing the process. This is important, as great candidates will be actively talking to a number of companies. If they have an interest in yours, you'll want them to hang in there for the process.

## The pressure interview

This interview will typically last 45 minutes. I call this the pressure interview because, once again, your role is not to make the person comfortable. That's his or her job. Your job is to be a guardian of the company. If possible, it is best to have two or three people from your company observe this interview. Note that I said to *observe*. I would have them take notes, but not actively participate in the interview.

Here is the format: Don't start with small talk. Be polite and direct. A great salesperson will have a desire to "work the room" and will establish the rapport or warmth of the session. Let the candidates do the work so you can see how effective they are at it. They'll likely do the same with your prospects. I will give you a few key building blocks to use for this interview. You will want to add your own important questions. I give you this script simply as a guide to plan your own interview. This interview is sometimes done via video.

"Thanks for coming in so quickly. As indicated during the phone screening, we've had a lot of interest in this role and we wanted to visit with some of the top candidates. I apologize in advance for moving quickly, but we only have 45 minutes, and there are so many things I'd like to learn."

"After this interview, we'll be asking you to verify your references and past earnings, and we'll quickly schedule a more traditional interview during which you can ask all sorts of questions you might have and tour the building. I know there is a lot you want to know about us, and we'll give you that opportunity to learn more at that time. Fair?"

"OK, before we get started: What is the one thing I should absolutely know about you if you are a part of my sales team, the one thing you want to make sure I don't leave this interview without understanding about you."

"Why did you pick that one?"

"Tell me about your current/most recent sales role."

"How do you prospect?" [Get details. How many, how often, what conversion rate, etc. Write down the answers. Be exact. Don't let anyone say 10 or 20 calls. How many is it? A great salesperson knows the numbers.]

"What are the stages of your process currently?" [Have the person give you conversion numbers for each stage.] You may have to guide him through this process to get numbers. For example:

- Fifty calls gives me ten appointments.
- Ten appointments get me three next steps.
- Three next steps get me two quotable projects and I close 50 percent.

"What's the length of your selling cycle?"

"How much is the size of the average sale?"

"Who is your competition?"

"How do you compare on price, quality, etc., with your competition?"

"What's something you wish you'd known when you started selling that product?"

"What's the biggest selling mistake you've made? What did it teach you?"

"How is your compensation structured?"

"How much did you sell last year?"

[Now that you have numbers, work backward with them as you calculate the "truthfulness" of the statements. For example: "So you sold $XXX,XXX? Based on the average size of your deals, that means you sold X clients, correct? So that's X deals per month? So you went on X calls, and X prospecting appointments. . . ."

[Usually you will find the numbers they claim regarding close rate and prospecting activities don't line up. Just say, "I'm puzzled why these aren't adding up? What am I missing?" Superstar salespeople won't be ruffled or fazed by this line. They'll just jump in and explain things. They might even, with some humor, say, "To be honest I don't track my numbers that closely; I just get results." A poser, a fake salesperson, will panic. You will see the difference clearly!]

"Walk me through the best sale you've done where you were in control from the very beginning of the sales process." [You don't want one that was in the pipeline when she took the role. Ask for lots of details and you'll discover how "real" the deal is and how large a role the person had in it. A salesperson can remember all the little facts about every deal he or she did. Don't let anyone use wishy-washy numbers. Be exact.]

"What do I need to know about your prospects?"

"OK, so I asked you to bring your sales material. Let's role play a typical sales visit you make. Who should I be?" [Role play as well as you can. Don't be tricky. Just like the phone screen, play a good prospect. The goal is to see what people's demeanor is. You want to see whether they use good questioning skills; tell stories to illustrate their points; speak concisely, displaying the skills of a Sales Star.]

"If you could go back and re-do that role play, what would you change?" [If you need to test the candidates' responsiveness to coaching, you might point out something that you didn't like about the role play and ask them to try again.]

"How do you like to be managed?"

"How do you organize and track your process?"

"What's something a past manager told you about your performance that you disagreed with at the time?"

"What has been your most effective way of learning new selling skills?"

[Ask a series of questions that relate to understanding their fit and experience against the criteria you placed in the posting. For instance, if your company sells to committees and does group presentations, have they done that recently and frequently? Probe regarding any job changes. Get the specifics regarding any claims of success you underlined previously in the person's résumé.]

Conduct this pressure exercise:

Ask the candidate to write down (preferably on a whiteboard in the front of the room) the top five qualities or habits he or she believes are critical to sales success. Don't comment on any of them yourself, just observe. Next ask the person to rank them in order of importance 1 through 5. Finally, pick whatever is number 4 and say, "I'm surprised that [number 4] wasn't in your top two. Why is that?" Again, the idea is simply to see how well the person articulates a position and handles stress. There is no right or wrong answer here, but would the way the candidate just responded be effective if he were selling to your prospects?

Once the candidate has left, ask the observers to sit quietly for the next ten minutes and write down a summary of everything they observed or felt about the candidate. It is important to do this without sharing your own opinion. People will tend to adjust their own views to match those of another person. Once everyone has written their observations, have them share them with the group. Decide whether you would like the process to continue with this candidate or not. Make the decision before leaving the room. If you've decided to move forward, contact the candidate the same day.

The next two steps, the performance interview and the romance interview, can often be combined into one event, the romance interview being dependent on how well the performance interview goes.

## The performance interview

The performance interview is the chance to see how the candidate will do in your company selling your product or service. You will provide the script, collateral, and a role-play scenario that mirrors one of the stages in your sales process. This might be the first face-to-face meeting with a new prospect or another part of your selling process that will allow you to see the candidate in action, as well as see how easily they learn and retain information. You will give the candidate a day or so to prepare and then ask that he or she role play the meeting with your team. You can download a sample of what this prep package might include at www.jonathanwhistman.com/thesalesboss.

Here's how to ask for the candidate's participation:

"[Name], we've really been impressed with what we've seen so far. Just so we can be really certain this is a product/ service that you'll enjoy selling and so we can get a feel for how you'd present things, I'd like to ask you to do one final thing before we make an offer. I'll provide the tools, scripts, and role-play setting. I'd like you to come in and sell to our team. I realize it won't be perfect and you won't have all the right answers, but we're OK if you make up a few things. We'd just like to see you in action. If that goes well, while you are here I'll give you a tour of the office, let you meet some of the rest of the team, and answer any questions you may have. When would you like to schedule this?"

During the few days the candidate takes to prep, I continue with a few other key processes to keep things moving along. For instance, now is the time to do the reference checks. You can ask the candidate to arrange the calls:

"While you're prepping for this final meeting, I'd like to have the opportunity to speak with [list of names from former companies]. Could you email them and ask them to connect with me? Thanks!"

The reason I ask that they arrange the calls is that sometimes it saves me from even calling the reference, as the salesperson says, "Well, actually he might not be the best person. . . ." When this happens, you know you haven't received the full truth during the interview. In cases where they say, "Sure, no problem!" I know what they told me was likely at least a version of the truth.

You will also conduct background screening if required at your company. This would also be a time to spend 20 minutes on Google. Google the person's name. Look carefully at his or her LinkedIn profile. Does everything add up with what you've been sold or told so far? I even consider looking at home addresses using Google Maps.

Read everything you can that the person has written online.

Some might find this extreme, but hey, if I'm investing over half a million dollars, I'll look for any clues I can to inform my decision.

On the day of the presentation, if possible, bring in a new set of employees to participate in this role play. You might even consider bringing in other members of the sales team to participate as buyers.

Once the presentation is complete, give some feedback to the candidate. Make sure to mention what he or she did well, but also point out one area that you know needs some work. This is an important step in determining how the person reacts to feedback. Is he or she open to growth?

Move directly to the next stage if appropriate. If everyone is on the same page regarding the candidate, you can do this the same day. Remember that in hiring a sales superstar, time is of the essence.

## The romance interview

This is finally the time when you get to try to woo the candidate into falling in love with your company. Pull out all the stops and let him or her visualize what being a part of the team would be like. Answer all the person's questions. Give a tour.

If possible, take the person out to eat somewhere unique. Say you'll be drawing up an offer. And then . . . pay attention. How does the person act at lunch when he or she believes the deal is done and there's no need to "sell" you? Don't miss this chance to observe. How does he treat the wait staff? That's how he'll treat your other employees. When you take someone out to eat, ask the person to drive. Don't go somewhere in walking distance. A salesperson will have prepared well for the meeting, but the unexpected "giving the new boss a ride" isn't part of the plan. You'd be surprised what you'll learn by getting in people's cars. Are they organized? Are they clean? Little clues. All are important.

● ● ●

This is your last chance to change your mind. Next, you'll be making the ultimate investment. There is one additional item that should be in place for you to have the best success when hiring and that is the use of scientific assessments. We'll look at why these are important in the next chapter.

# 8

# Use the Power of Science in Selection

Humans have for ages tried to use science to understand the behaviors and actions of people, with various levels of success. Going back to Greek times, the physician Galen popularized the idea that people were influenced by their blood types; the Chinese believed that the year of a person's birth influenced who he or she was; and almost every society since has had ways of categorizing people. Fortunately for us, the science of human behavior has come a long way and it now is absolutely possible to predict human behavior using scientific assessments.

It is critical that your company use a scientific assessment tool to complete the picture of the potential sales candidate to ensure you are making the best possible decision. I'm addressing the topic in this chapter at the end of the process of hiring, although the use of assessments and its actual place in the hiring process could be before the phone screen, before the first interview, after the first interview, or in conjunction with the performance interview. Typically, the earlier in the process you use an assessment tool, the better, as it prevents you from becoming emotionally attached to a candidate the tool indicates is a bad fit. The reason companies might choose to wait until later in the process is to control their costs. A company should expect to invest between $250 and $400 per serious candidate in assessment costs.

What can you expect from an assessment tool? An assessment is based on proven science. In order to be utilized for hiring, the testing providers must certify the assessment tool through a process of predictive validity. This simply means they have to prove the tool and its results accurately measure what they say it does. Brain and human sciences have come a long way in the last five years. Hiring without an assessment is simply irresponsible. It would almost be like hiring a sales guy without allowing him email and a cell phone. He might still be able to sell, but he sure would be handicapped! A good assessment tool will measure the candidates' fit in your environment, their learning styles, and the best way to manage and motivate them. Plus it will offer a whole host of other critical data points. I personally have had great success using PXT Select and Everything DiSC. You can learn more about them through our resource page if you registered for access to additional resources at www.jonathanwhistman.com/thesalesboss.

Because there is a wide range of assessment tools on the market, it is important that you understand some of the key things that these tools can provide. I like to think of these tools as allowing us to see the how and the why someone will perform in a certain capacity. Let's consider the power and use of these two tools.

The PXT Select will help you understand how a person thinks and communicates in comparison to the population as a whole. It measures verbal skill, verbal reasoning, numerical ability, and numerical reasoning and lets us understand a person's thinking style. It isn't an intelligence test, but simply lets us know how the person learns and communicates. You can think of it as having two different containers that each hold five gallons of water. One might be a narrow-mouth vase, while the second is a five-gallon bucket. Both of them would hold the same amount of water, but you'd have to pour the water in at different rates! Imagine if you knew your new salesperson was the five-gallon bucket with the ability to learn really quickly. Or what if your selling environment and company needed slow, steady training before putting salespeople into the field? The key is in understanding what the person is like in comparison to the environment you will place him or her into. The assessment also looks at pace, assertiveness, sociability, conformity, outlook, decisiveness, accommodation, independence, and judgment. You can see these things are critical to understand about the potential hire and how difficult they'd be to measure without an assessment, simply relying on interviewing techniques. Your PXT Select partner will help you establish a "job pattern" that reflects the skills you are looking for in a person selling in your environment, for your industry, and with your product.

The second type of assessment is the Everything DiSC. Have you ever wondered why you seem to understand and relate to some people better than to others? The science of DiSC has been helping people better understand themselves and how they react to the environment around them for more than 40 years. When using tools such as this, it is important to note that a DiSC-based assessment doesn't tell you whether a person CAN or WILL do the job; it simply tells you what that person's behavior will look like within the team. Because this is the case, you wouldn't use the DiSC to determine a fit in the role, but rather the fit into your existing team and what might be the best approach in terms of training, coaching, and managing the person once hired.

It is my belief that every Sales Boss should be an expert in the science of DiSC. Its research-validated model will allow you to get the best results from the energy and effort you put into leading the team. It will increase your understanding of yourself and your impact on the people around you and elevate your understanding of how to achieve results through people. I'll cover some of the key attributes in the remainder of this chapter; if you see value in this science, you should identify and work with a provider of Everything DiSC. I've included some sources at www.jonathanwhistman/thesalesboss.

The term DiSC comes from the acronym formed from the behavior tendencies measured: Dominance, Influence, Steadiness, and Conscientiousness. You can expect someone with a high-D style to be more direct, results-oriented, firm, strong-willed, and forceful than someone who is high-S. A high-S might be described as a person who is even-tempered, accommodating, patient, humble, and tactful. The high-I would be outgoing, enthusiastic, optimistic, and lively. The high-C would be the opposite, showing traits such as being analytical, reserved, precise, private, and systematic. Understanding the preferred environment of your sales hire and correlating it with the environment he or she will be asked to sell into is a key to improving your hiring success.

A good team will have people who come from a variety of behavior styles so that the team is well rounded and appeals to a broad section of potential customers. For instance if your selling environment requires strict attention to detail, facts and figures, and spreadsheets, then you would do well to have someone with some of the C traits. If you need someone who is out at tradeshows meeting people every day, then you might do better selecting an I trait. Remember that these styles are just preferences and not indications of how anyone will perform. You first need to make sure the person can sell and then, all else being equal, pick the candidate who most closely aligns to the sales environment. You might also pair people up with prospects who share their styles and teach them how to adapt their selling styles. This would be under the premise that people like to buy from people like themselves. Beyond the hiring process, these tools will also inform how you coach, mentor, or train your people.

Don't ever plan to hire someone without making use of the latest that science has to offer, but also recognize that an assessment tool is only part of the complete picture and you must run every other portion of the process well in order to have the best results.

If you have carefully executed the process outlined in the previous chapter, you can be confident that you have hired a sales superstar. Just remember that even a superstar can fail in the wrong environment. Be just as diligent in the crafting and execution of the on-boarding process.

CHAPTER

9

# On-Boarding a New Member of the Sales Team

The way you bring salespeople into your team has a profound impact on the success they will have selling for your company. Remember that we all tend to change our habits to fit the environment we are in. Recall the clean and dirty bathrooms we mentioned earlier? If you've followed the hiring process that was outlined in the previous chapters, you have already gone a long way toward communicating with the new hire that he is joining a sales team that operates at a very high level. Let's not spoil that impression on the first day!

Any required HR paperwork should have been emailed to new hires prior to the first day or can be handled later. Never allow a candidate's first day to start with a visit to Human Resources. If this is your company's policy, fight to have it changed. If you can't change it, you should be in HR with the person and make sure the process isn't boring or irrelevant. Get your person in and out as quickly as possible!

The first day and weeks of any new people's arrival at your company should be orchestrated and planned to help cement the idea in the candidates' minds that they made the right decision to spend the next part of their careers with your team and should infuse within them your standards for performance. Because the circumstances of each company will be different, some hiring salespeople who work out of the office, some from home, some from the field, and some on the phone, I will simply give you general guidelines that you should apply to your process.

First, everything should be ready in advance. What does it say to new hires if they show up and have to wait in the lobby, if their computers aren't available for a few days, or they don't have business cards? Sloppy and careless leaders run the show here! It isn't a surprise that they are starting that day, so make sure everything is buttoned up and ready.

One of my clients came to me with a concern about the high level of turnover in a very short period after hiring a new salesperson. They asked for help in figuring out how to improve the retention rate. I looked at what happened during those first few days. The company's salespeople sold throughout the United States and worked from their home offices. They traveled by car to the places within their territories. When new people were hired, they were asked to fly to the company's headquarters to receive their training and orientation.

Here was my experience as I traced one person's onboarding. He flew into the airport and got a taxi to the hotel that was reserved for him by the company. The hotel was a Motel 6 equivalent. In the morning, he had instructions to show up to Building 10 at 8 a.m. and ask for the Human Resources department, where there would be another group of new hires (not all salespeople). When he arrived at 7:45 a.m., there was nobody around, so he waited in the lobby. The lobby was dirty, with magazines that were six months out of date. The first HR staff person finally showed up at 8 a.m. and hurriedly introduced herself, saying it would be a few minutes before she was ready. By this time, five additional new hires were waiting in the lobby. Around 8:15, the HR staff member reappeared and took everyone to a conference room. On the way, the HR person complained and apologized about how hectic things were. She explained that the first person on the agenda for the orientation that morning seemed to have forgotten, so they were trying to shuffle things around and see whether one of the other presenters could start earlier than planned.

I'll spare you the remaining details. It went downhill from there. Two days of long, boring HR paperwork and all the required sexual harassment training, and so on, were checked off the list. During the week, no dinners were planned—just a cold lunch provided in the training room. What do you think the sales guy thought of his choice to join the company?

It took an additional week after he arrived home to get his computer and sales collateral. Then it took a full month to receive his business cards. He was instructed just to mark out the last guy's name in the meantime and pencil in his contact information! Was it any wonder he didn't stay long and the company continued to have high turnover?

We redesigned the process. The small details add up to a big impression. Here was the new process: Before traveling to the new hire orientation week, the new salesperson received a personal call from his or her new manager, welcoming the person and talking through the itinerary for the week ahead. The managers would also make it their mission to get personal details that they usually would not have asked of the candidates in an interview: Were they married, did they have kids, any hobbies, and so forth? These details would become useful later.

The new hire received a welcome package in the mail with branded company gear, a handwritten welcome-aboard note from the CEO, and a gift card for a restaurant in his or her hometown to take the family out before leaving for the week. Is this better already? The welcome gets better!

Once the salesperson arrived at the airport, a driver was waiting with his or her name on a sign, helped with the baggage, and then the person was whisked off to one of the nicer hotels in town, close to all the action. The driver said he'd be back in the morning at a specific time to go to the company's headquarters.

Upon entering the hotel room, the new salesperson would see a care package in the room. It included an iPad with all the instructions to get into the company's email system. When the new salesperson logged into email, the inbox already had welcome-aboard messages from the rest of the sales team and other department heads! The iPad played an emotional welcome video that explained the history of the company and some of the core principles. Also in the care package, besides the chocolates, were business cards, a fine ink pen, and a paper tablet. Trainees received laptops when they arrived at the training in the morning.

The day started with a tour of all of the production spaces and meeting some of the key staff. The day even included a trip out to see the equipment they'd be selling installed at a customer's location.

While they were busy that day, a care package was sent to the employees' homes addressed to the family, perhaps a spouse, maybe some children. This package contained a "Thanks for lending us your spouse!" card and some other small gifts, such as movie tickets, a gift card to Toys-R-Us, or a basket of goodies related to what was of interest to the family. What do you think the difference in attitude and energy was when the salesperson called home after the first night of training in the second example versus the first? I can just imagine the family at home saying, "Don't mess this one up! It sounds like you've found the right place!"

And from here it continued to get better. Suffice it to say that every moment of that training was well planned and orchestrated. The turnover rate in the sales team quickly plunged to below 10 percent.

What is the first impression of your company on the salesperson's first days? Outside of the crafting of the environment, there are also things to accomplish regarding learning the product, computer systems, internal company functions, and more. Largely, the type of company and the complexity of the sale will determine how you handle this initial training period, but a key guideline to follow is to integrate some selling activity as soon as possible. Don't wait until someone is fully trained. Remember that habits are powerful. Have you ever been in a good fitness routine of eating and exercise and then had it interrupted by a long vacation followed by a heavy workload? How hard was it to get back into the healthy fitness habits? Use this same understanding when thinking about keeping your new salesperson's selling skills in top shape. You hire people you know are in fit shape; don't let them lose these habits during a long training process. Get them right into new habits.

Some ways you might sprinkle in sales activity throughout the training period are:

1. Have them call their old clients and set up introductory meetings with your team. This keeps them in prospecting mode and doesn't require them to be experts. If they've had good client relationships in the past, it'll be easy to persuade their former clients to do them a favor and see your company. Next, have the new hire accompany your best salesperson on the actual call. A word of caution: Don't embarrass the new salesperson with his old clients by having him go on the call with a mediocre salesperson. This will destroy his faith in your team. Pair him with someone who will awe him with his or her skill.

2. After learning about a product, have the new hire role play a sales call with your team. Your team will be potential customers for whom the product the salesperson has just learned about is the appropriate solution.

3. Have them do sales ride-alongs with a team member. Have them handle all of the data entry into the customer relationship management (CRM) software. This will help them learn the computer systems using real scenarios rather than just classroom knowledge. If you do this, you'll see a higher adoption rate of the CRM once they are in the field.

4. Have them analyze their assigned territory and create a prospecting and customer development plan. Where will they travel? How will they prioritize their activity? This will allow you to see how they think and cause them to be excited to get in the game.

5. Have them teach a segment at one of your regularly scheduled sales meetings. Assign topics such as phone prospecting, handling objections, effective use of questions, or some other critical selling skills. They will present a teaching segment to the sales team. The sales team will give them feedback. This allows you to see how they think about the topic, how well they present and hold the attention of the group, and keeps their skills sharp.

There are many other ways to add in selling activity before the completion of their training. Spend some time planning what these are and be intentional with the implementation. Where possible, don't have a day pass by that they don't spend some of it exercising the same skills you need them to display when they are finally turned loose on their own. Use your imagination to supercharge each activity by adding a twist that makes it more memorable, impactful, and fun and that keeps their selling juices going. Don't allow mental laziness. Set the standard that to be a part of your group means that they will continue to learn and increase their knowledge base of your field, including your competition. You don't expect them to be experts on day one; you do, however, expect that they'll continue to grow each day, even if they are with the company for twenty years. Old dogs can and will learn new tricks.

As an example, several of my clients sell capital equipment: large-scale automated packaging equipment. These are complex machines, going into complex manufacturing and processing environments. Even with a background in the industry, a new salesperson has a lot to learn! The best companies stagger the learning expectations and, importantly, test that the salesperson has retained the knowledge. Let's take a thermoforming machine as an example. The first phase of learning expectations might be:

- What is a thermoforming machine?
- How does it work?
- Why do our customers use it?
- What problems are we uniquely qualified to fix for our customers?
- How much does it cost?
- What is the lead time from order to delivery?
- Who is the ideal customer for this piece of equipment?
- How was it done before thermoforming?

That might be enough for them to learn and pass a test on in the first thirty days. Perhaps a similar test for each key piece of equipment they'll be responsible for selling could be developed.

What about at the end of their first quarter with the company? Perhaps you expect they'll have increased their knowledge with:

- Who are our main competitors on the thermoforming machine?
- How do I conduct an ROI discussion with the prospect?
- What is the typical payback period?
- What are the alternative methods of packaging that compete with ours for this type of process?
- How do our machines differ from the competition and why?

At the end of the second quarter:

- What are the names of the salespeople at our competitors who sell in your territory?

- Who are their key customers?
- What equipment comes before and after our thermoformer in the production line?
- Who sells these other pieces of equipment?

At the end of the fourth quarter, you add to the list. No mental laziness is allowed on your team. You set the tone that, in addition to filling the sales role, you expect that they will be progressively and intentionally increasing their knowledge. You will verify this through some test that verifies they are doing so. School is never out for a professional on your team.

How can you test their knowledge? You might use written tests, causal interviews, peer reviews, or some other method. The real key is that it must be formalized and expected. Nothing is left to chance on the A-team.

Sometimes you might find when you take on the sales manager role that there is not a good training library. If this is the case, create one quickly. This is an area where you shouldn't allow wanting perfection to keep you from starting to develop a library. You can always improve it over time, but it is critical that you start with something as soon as possible.

One method that might be helpful is to have your product experts or product managers walk you through the intricacies of the product your team sells. Video-record everything! Ask them to list the top 20 things a person needs to know and be able to speak intelligently about. Ask your experienced salespeople to tell you what they think is critical, and be sure to get some video of this information. Don't just focus on "how this product works"; also focus on the "why." What problem does it solve for our customers and how? Remember the old selling routine of FAB: feature-advantage-benefit. This X has this feature, and the advantage of this is it reduces XYZ, and the benefit to our customer is ABC. Once you have these videos, use them to create mini-lessons. Split them into segments that correspond to the quarter or period in which you have set your learning expectations for the new salesperson.

Your training library should also have full-length sales calls that the salesperson can view as a standard of what excellence looks like. If there are several stages of calls, each of them should have a video. Record a role play with your best salespeople.

If you don't have the company resources to edit the videos into something appealing, consider outsourcing the creation. I have used Upwork.com with great success. You can post a request, upload the videos and a list of the key learning points. You will receive a fully produced learning product complete with overlays, music, and other features. You can even state what you are willing to pay if you have a limited budget or time constraints. If you want to maximize your time return, choose someone in another time zone to do the editing. This allows you to view what they have done; they'll work on it while you are sleeping and you'll have the work the next day when you come back into the office. The key is to finish the videos and put them into the hands of your new salesperson.

If you have a new person starting, and you don't have training videos ready, then have the employee record everything he or she sees during the first month! If someone is walking her through a product, record it! If he is attending a sales presentation, record it! You can then use these videos in the future.

If you must do this creation work yourself, I recommend using a product called Camtasia. Check them out on the web and you'll see how easy it is to create great content. Of course, you have more important work to do, so opt to have someone else do the creative work if at all possible. Just remember, at the end of the day it is your fault! If you don't have what you need, you must get it. The idea is not to create extra work. Use the things already happening and capture them for training re-use in the future. For instance, if your team is presenting at a trade show and they do a walk-through of the equipment they are selling before the show, simply think ahead about how to capture it effectively for training purposes.

Once you have some training collateral, find a way to automate its distribution and the testing. There are learning management systems (LMSs) that can be used to offer access to the training. You could also simply schedule emails to go out with the links to the proper training. These emails could be in 60-, 90-, or 120-day increments to encourage and promote continual learning. Set a reminder in your calendar (this also can be automated!) to follow up with the skills test. Any good customer relationship management (CRM) program can add automation to routine activities. For salespeople, I like these tests largely to take the form of role-playing sales scenarios with peers who can do a peer review. This not only tests knowledge acquisition but also reinforces good selling behavior. After all, it's not just knowledge for knowledge's sake, but it is to help them sell more effectively.

A side note: When you conduct a role play, record it. Give it to the salesperson to view. Most of us have never watched ourselves on a regular basis in a sales task. You'll be surprised at the improvements they'll make as they regularly see themselves. Remember when we talked about things being good or bad by comparison? This is a great opportunity to give them something to compare themselves to when rating their performance.

Once you have set up a process of training that leaves no room for mental laziness, you will find that the results start to improve. Great salespeople have a bit of a competitive nature, and they'll thrive in this environment. Unfortunately, the old truism "If you don't use it you lose it" is also at play. Build a method into your automated routine that encourages the team to revisit and relearn important topics. Fortunately, there are companies that sell products to facilitate this.

One such company is Mindmarker. Mindmarker will take your content and create follow-up reminders, quizzes, and activities and distribute these to your team right onto their smart phones at spaced intervals to reinforce their learning. They can revisit in quarter three something you taught in quarter one. You will know how well information is being used and retained. These types of products come complete with dashboards so you can see at a glance how people are doing and the level of participation. The cost is typically reasonable per user, so no reason exists not to use them or something similar if you don't have something already in place.

Nobody likes to be micro-managed. Having a robust and automated training system allows you to have this critical function on autopilot. Your involvement is minimized to times when someone really goes off course or just needs small adjustments and encouragement.

Once you set ongoing training as a Sacred Rhythm in your organization, people will expect it and will not bristle at participating. They'll view it simply as a way your team stays in top shape and beats the competition. Compare this to the manager who only gets involved and digs into the details when he's unhappy with a team member! When you only have random inspections and manager involvement, then the salespeople will feel micro-managed and isolated. It'll be like a bird swooped in and pooped on them. They'll immediately feel like they are doing something wrong and become defensive. So make it easy on yourself. Set an early expectation on how they'll grow their abilities. Even on a pro sports team everyone hits the practice field to improve and learn how to play with the team during the next critical game. Take it to the next level and offer badges, prizes, and drawings for participants. There has been a lot of research into gamification that shows how much more deeply engaged people are, both in the level of effort and time, when there is a "game" aspect of the technology. Many modern CRM systems have this ability built into their platforms, but if that is not possible for you, then simply create more awareness by openly publishing results and celebrating success.

One CEO of a company that has been my client is outstanding in this regard. He even created an official-looking passport that was given to new hires. They would have their "visas" stamped in their passports as they achieved certain company milestones, experiences, or training levels. Get out of the typical training mindset and find a way to make it engaging, fun, and self-reinforcing.

CHAPTER

# 10

# Know Your Sales Process and Your Numbers

What creates success for a salesperson at your company? Where do leads usually come from? How do they progress from interest to sale? When I ask this of mediocre sales managers, I am often told: "It depends; every case is a little different." When I probe a little deeper, this is usually code for "I don't teach a system." In *every* case, it is a sure sign that the team is underperforming.

As a manager of the team, you must not only know the typical selling processes but you must also understand the numbers around these processes and have a strong opinion about what works and why. You will allow individual flexibility, but you need also to teach a system for selling. Yes, every case is a little different. Yes, every salesperson has unique quirks, personality, talents, and magic. You must, however, sort through all of this to have a road map to give your team. You will set the standard, and you'll decide how much deviation from the standard is acceptable as the team adds their quirks, personality, talents, and magic.

I think of a sales process and the people charged with carrying it out like a serial TV show. The topic and style of successful shows take many different formats, but all of them share some basic DNA. Think about a successful TV series. They all have:

- A premise or overarching plot line. Think: Crime scene investigator takes justice into his hands by vigilante murders. The premise must be "big enough" to handle the variety of episodes within the series.
- Each episode contributes to the plot line and hooks the watcher into tuning in again next week.
- Each episode begins with a summary of the season to date.

- They have characters who act in a predictable (and sometimes predictably unpredictable) ways.
- They have music and imagery that immediately brings up a fondness for the series. Sometimes just hearing the opening musical notes can produce a flood of emotion. Think: *Star Wars, Mission Impossible,* or *Survivor.*

Thinking of your sales process as a TV series is an effective way to teach and mentor the team and also gain clarity. In many of the companies I work with, the sales managers think they have a sales process, but when the team is asked to write down the sales stages, there is no agreement. In one company, the number of steps ranged from three all the way to thirteen depending on the sales rep. Let's look at this in action:

1. Prospecting
2. Initial contact
3. First sales visit on phone
4. In-person visit and qualification
5. Tour customer's production plant
6. Create samples
7. Gain agreement
8. Present proposal
9. Negotiate details
10. Sign agreement

This might represent a typical salesperson's sales process. Because they have achieved success with this series of "episodes," they continue to do it this way. Another salesperson might combine and eliminate steps, and the process becomes:

1. Prospecting
2. Initial phone contact qualification

3. Customer visit and plant (or office) tour
4. Create consensus, negotiate details
5. Sign agreement

The differences may not seem important, but they are! Some processes add unnecessary steps, create delays, raise objections the prospect hadn't even thought of, and much more. You'll discover some sell almost completely by email; some do the proposal in person, some over the phone. Some start with the fee, while others wait to discuss fees until the end. I'm not suggesting which series of episodes above is more effective, but I am suggesting that there is a truth contained within the experience of your team that can be of use to you. Your job is to find and define the best practice. If you want to enlighten yourself, try this exercise: Ask each member of your team to write out the stages in his or her personal sales process. Compare notes.

Once you have your company's processes, you will want to define each episode/stage. Think of the episode definition as the little explainer text you see on Netflix about what the viewer can expect. You are defining what happens in this episode. How does it tie into the previous episode? How does it build momentum? How does it end so the prospect tunes into the next episode? What imagery and tone will attract the sale?

I like to be creative and write it out as an actual story: "The customers enter our facility and are wowed by our attention to detail. As they sit sipping their coffee, they notice . . . as they see our demo, they . . . and so forth. They leave understanding the power of our operation and eager to discover how it will impact their current. . . ."

Be dramatic. People love, learn, and remember stories. Your salespeople are people. You want them emotionally "getting" what their task is as it relates to the customer at each phase. What is the journey they should be taking their prospects on through their sales process? Writing out a customer story will allow you to know how to title this episode of the customer journey from prospect to the sale. What are the stories your salespeople are telling in the field? You might have noticed when we labeled the parts of the hiring process we called them the *pressure interview* and the *romance interview*. After you learned these hiring skills, the name of the stage alone reminds you of what the key is to success at that phase of the process.

A new salesperson joining your company should clearly understand the series and the importance of each episode. Outside of TV, in the world of sports, top athletes have a system. They have a way to approach the ball, serve, hit, stance, and so on. It is only by having a system that they know how to diagnose what is going wrong and how to get better. It is similar with your team. If they are going to get better, you can't have every "at-bat" be completely different.

The look, feel, and substance of interactions should carry the company's image. The art of great sales management means you do this in a way that allows freedom of the individual's quirks, personality, talent, and magic. If you are not careful, in a quest for consistency, you can squeeze out the human traits that add power to the process. It's a tough balance to achieve, but one that a high EQ manager will excel at.

Now that you understand the importance of mastering and publishing a company's sales process, it is equally important that you know the numbers. What is the conversion between stages? How much of each phase of activity leads to the right pipeline? How much pipeline is needed to produce the sales numbers? This is critical. You and every member of the team must know the numbers. At the end of the day, sales matters, but it is in the data of those dollars that future riches lie. It is the clue to where to mine for gold.

We'll talk about how to use the numbers, but a few words of caution now:

1. When you focus strictly on numbers, salespeople will feel micro-managed. Numbers only tell part of the story. Never diagnose with numbers. Use numbers as a symptom and a clue of where to look when there are struggles.
2. No salesperson likes paperwork, so your systems must gather the metrics without creating extra or redundant work.
3. The numbers must be real to them to have meaning and impact. Don't manage strictly by the numbers or independently set behavior metrics. Meaning, don't just pick numbers out of the air and expect salespeople to achieve them. They've got to understand how you arrived at the numbers.
4. Don't start a discussion with a number, for example: "I noticed in the CRM that you didn't do many prospecting phone calls this week." Be human. Only reference the numbers in a real conversation that is tied to their motivation and results.

## The Numbers That Matter

We've indicated previously that a great salesperson knows his or her numbers. As the Sales Boss, you must know the numbers of each person on the team. This is an area where a one-size-fits-all approach doesn't work. You'll need to understand how the skill of each person impacts the numbers that you will be measuring. Most of the numbers you will have as data inside your CRM, discussed in greater detail in Chapter 16. I've heard many sales managers state that the only number they care about is the final sales number, and that if a person is "making the number" then that is all that counts.

This is not the view of a Sales Boss. You will want to be familiar with all of the metrics that drive the number. Only by understanding the numbers of even your best performers will you be in the position to influence the results or understand whether you are maximizing the potential of the team. The key is balance. Don't become overly focused on the data to the detriment of your people skills, but also don't rely strictly on your people skills and ignore the numbers. Here are the critical key numbers you must know. For each of them you should know the company average and each person's absolute number individually.

- What is the total target sales revenue number? The quota?
- What is the average size deal or how many deals make up that number historically?
- What is the absolute closing percentage from the quota (or similar) stage?
- What is the fall-out number between each stage leading up to the close?
- How many prospecting emails, phone calls, visits, or activities?
- How many company-provided leads?
- What is the velocity of each stage?
- What is the "target pipeline value" expectation?

Knowing these numbers is not micro-management; it is good business and the mark of the Sales Boss. Let's discuss the importance of these numbers and how we arrive at them. If a salesperson has a quota of $2 million in sales and closes 30 percent of the deals quoted, how much quote volume should that person have running in his or her pipeline? Roughly, $7 million should be accounted for if he or she expects to achieve quota.

You can figure the pipeline number by the dollar amount or by the number of deals needed if you have similar size deals. In the previous case, if an average deal is $100,000 a salesperson will need to close 20 deals but would need 70 showing in the pipeline at all times. This would become your metric for target pipeline value. This number should be discussed during your pipeline review meetings, which we outline in Chapter 13. What if a salesperson closes 50 percent? Well, you can see how the total pipeline value would reflect the skill of that salesperson. The total pipeline value metric should always be done on an individual level, using actual historical data based on the person's results. The only time this would not be true is when you have a new person starting and thus have no individual data. In this case you'd clearly tell the person what percentage you are using and that this number comes from an aggregate of the team's historical performance.

Next, understanding the fall-out between stages leading up to each stage of the sale is important. For instance, take these scenarios:

*Salesperson 1:* Makes 20 phone calls to a prequalified targeted list and sets ten face-to-face appointments, resulting in three opportunities to quote.

*Salesperson 2:* Makes 20 phone calls to a prequalified targeted list and sets five face-to-face appointments, resulting in three opportunities to quote.

If you were looking at these numbers, what diagnoses could you make? That's a trick question. You can't make a diagnosis, but you can develop a theory about what might be happening and use this to coach and later diagnose.

For instance, with Salesperson 1, perhaps he is not doing a skillful job on the phone uncovering situations that would disqualify a prospect, thus spending more unproductive time in face-to-face meetings. An alternative theory might be that he is great on the phone, but when he gets face-to-face he lacks the presence and power to move to the quote stage. The point is, the data will only tell you so much, but once you know what the team averages are and the individual's results, then you know where to look. If you know that the team averages setting appointments with 45 percent of the dials made, it is likely that someone operating at 30 percent could use some additional training on phone skills. The context adds meaning. Make certain that you know the fall-out between each stage and why it is happening.

Velocity of each stage means how quickly a prospect of a certain type and size moves through your process. Does it take a week from getting the lead to holding a face-to-face meeting? Does the next stage happen over 30 days or 60? Knowing this metric allows you and your salesperson to do a couple of things. First, it highlights opportunities that might be neglected and need some attention. If someone usually takes 30 days to review a proposal or digest information, and this deal is already at 60 days, what does that tell you? Knowing the velocity number allows you to plan your time so things don't slip through the cracks. Remember the motto in sales: Time kills all deals, even the good ones. Meaning: The more unnecessary time you allow to pass, the greater the chance that something can go wrong and the deal will never close.

Another benefit of knowing velocity is knowing when a deal is over or unlikely. This can keep salespeople from spending time chasing deals that have a very small chance of closing and spend their time on more profitable prospects. It allows you as the Sales Boss to remove some of the bloat that builds up in a team member's forecast. Salespeople hate to call a deal dead, and that's usually a good quality except when it gives them or the company a false sense of security by seeing that deal still in the pipeline. If it's outside the velocity zone, consider removing it from the forecast.

Finally, understand the number and size of the efforts related to prospecting. Much of this data can be obtained automatically through the CRM without much additional documentation effort. The future sales of your team are tied to today's prospecting activity. It is a leading indicator of your future results. What typically happens is that a salesperson looks at the sales number or pipeline and, realizing that it is empty or not up to par, starts prospecting. He or she turns over every rock in the desire to get something started and to keep from starving. As a result, salespeople issue some quotes, then start relaxing and following up on those quotes. They close some deals, and they relax into servicing and delivering to these new customers, and in the meantime, the prospecting is neglected, the funnel gets skinny, and they are staring once again at an anemic forecast. The cure for this is consistent prospecting, even when things are good and you are busy. Know the prospecting number and stick to it. In fact, I always suggest salespeople name their best customer "Prospecting," because they'd never dream of neglecting their best customer.

The best rewards come from prospecting, and prospecting is the most consistently paying customer! Don't let your team neglect it. Know the number that creates the individual results and highlight the importance of achieving that number. I have a client who created what they called the Easy Button on their CRM dashboard. Every day when a salesperson logs in, it is filled with precisely the number of prospecting activities needed pre-loaded with names and numbers. The Easy Button helped establish a Sacred Rhythm of prospecting.

Assist salespeople to know what their numbers should be. You can work backward from results to behavior. If a person needs to sell X and closes Y, then he needs to quote Z. If he produces a quote with every X number of visits and it takes X number of emails/calls to get a visit, then he knows how many emails and phone calls he should be making. This should be a daily number. It really is no different than how the business operates or how a family budget works. It is inputs and outputs. Help the salespeople understand what the dollar figure is for getting out of bed each day in terms of cost of living and future dreams, and then tie this as closely to the activity metric as possible and you will see the power of motivation kick in. This is the power of knowing your sales process and the numbers.

something. Step in when a star is creating animosity or a corrosive environment, but most of the time just clear the path for him. When you need the stars to follow a rule or a process, you'll need to help them appreciate the impact it has on their results or the results of the company. Most stars also have an altruistic side that can be co-opted into polishing the other team members.

Carefully prod the thinking of the stars to realize that they aren't yet where they could be and that they can improve. Their competitive nature will fuel their fire. The best sales stars end up competing, even with themselves. They love to win for winning's sake. It might be better to say they hate losing more than they love winning. If the selling skills of your stars surpass your abilities (and this is likely the case), get them some outside coaching that isn't given to the entire group. For instance, you might have the entire sales team participate in monthly sales training, and you might have an outside trainer come in to teach the group throughout the year. By its nature, these group sessions are simplified to accommodate the wide range of talents on the team.

Pick something special for your stars to experience outside of the group environment. That means if the whole team is star players you'd pick something different for each player. An example might be sending them to a personal development Tony Robbins–style seminar or some high-level event that they might not pay for themselves. The event does not have to be related to selling. Choose something that will stretch their views of what is possible in life and that energizes them for growth. If you've developed a relationship with them, you are likely to know what type of events would provide this stimulus. Remember when we said "Things are only good or bad by comparison"? Your star players compare themselves to everyone on the team. They see that they are at the top and plateau unless you provide them something bigger. In most cases, this point of comparison must come from outside your company. A bonus of providing them these opportunities is that their affinity for you will grow as a result. They'll not just see you as a manager, but as an ally. If you give bonuses that are strictly cash, the bonus will soon be forgotten. If, however, you use experiences as a bonus, they will not only remember the experiences for years, but you will also be energizing them for better performance.

Wise managers set aside time to nourish the stars on the team. They also spend time with the up-and-coming talent. They clear the deck of anyone who consistently fails to improve. It isn't worth the time. Be willing to sit in judgment.

Think of it like this: If you had a job that required a dog, but you couldn't easily find any dogs, would you go out and buy a cat? The reality is that even if (after a lot of effort and time) you could get the cat to bark like a dog, it'd never be that convincing. Both have four legs and fur, but nobody mistakes one for the other! In sales, you also need a certain DNA. If you hire someone without it, no amount of coaching and mentoring will get the person to be convincing (or successful) in the sales role. Start with the dog, the right sales DNA, and then train the person to be the best dog.

Who are the cats on your team right now? If you look at these cats and know they'll never be convincing sales stars, then do something sooner rather than later. The question isn't "Can they sell?" The real question is "Can they sell like stars?" Don't keep a cat. If you don't have any C-players on your team (cats), then it's easy to spend time with the right people: your stars and up-and-coming stars.

• • •

In the next few chapters, we'll progress through how you should spend your time with your team, what meetings you absolutely must have, and then how best to play the role of coach, mentor, and leader—how to be the ultimate Sales Boss.

# Team Rhythms That Lead to Group Cohesion

We've discussed establishing some Sacred Rhythms that will help you in your management and motivation of the team. Let's discuss what some of those key rhythms need to be for your team. A team cannot operate effectively together without regular meetings. It is essential that you hold regular and productive meetings. Understand that if you run a poor meeting, you'll get poor results and people will believe you are wasting their time.

I suggest that you take an anonymous vote at least twice yearly to see whether the participants of the meeting think you should keep the meeting or get rid of it. Do a vote any time you personally feel the energy has left the meeting. If a majority feel the meeting should be axed, then the next meeting should be started something like this:

> "Well, the results are in, and 75 percent of you think this meeting should be axed and is a waste of your time. My apologies! I guess I haven't done my job well enough in making sure this meeting provides value to you. I hate wasting your time, as I know you have important selling activities to be involved in today. I have this meeting scheduled because I believe it's important to _____ . So the question is: How can we change this meeting to accomplish that goal and provide enough value so that next time you vote to keep this meeting? Let's spend the remainder of our time figuring that out."

Then have an open discussion on what would make the meeting better and more effective. This type of honest communication will send the message to your team that you value them, that you don't want to micro-manage, and that results are important. It will also allow you to customize your meetings to achieve results. Remember, these meetings are sacred, so I would never actually cancel them. I'd just work to repurpose them into something useful.

I'd like to share a meeting facilitation technique that you can use in a variety of ways, but that will prove effective specifically in this setting. Have you ever needed to ask for the group's input and then had one person dominate the discussion or had the discussion go in so many directions there is no clear answer as to the action to be taken? If so, this meeting technique will help. I learned it in a Crestcom Leadership class. They call it the one-third plus one technique, but it has been taught in many other iterations under other names.

Start the meeting by defining the problem for the group. In this case, it would be: "We need to make this meeting more valuable." Next, give the team five minutes of silent thinking time and ask them to write down solutions or problems with the meeting. You pick: Do you want to hear problems that should be eliminated or solutions? Maybe you'll do both, but start with one. Ask them to circle their top three to five (you choose the number) thoughts. Having them write something down keeps the meeting moving and also keeps one strong voice from influencing everyone else.

When the five minutes are up, go around the room having people share *one* item each. Continue to go around the room until everyone's top items have been shared. As the group is sharing, someone should be writing the list on a flip chart (or using some other method if this is an online call).

Number the list, starting at number 1 and going through the end of the list. Once you have a total number of items, divide the number into thirds and add one. For instance, if you have twelve items on the list, you would divide it into thirds (four) and add one, giving you five. Five is the number of votes each participant is allowed.

Go quickly around the room, with each person placing five votes for what he or she thinks are the top items to consider (1, 2, 6, 8, 9), using just the number designation. The facilitator tallies the marks on the flip chart and then comes up with a total for each category.

At the end, you will typically have a consensus on the top three items that can be actionable. Start the discussion here. You might even choose to do another round on the highest rated item, this time changing the premise to asking how to implement or change the item under discussion. You can see a video example of this technique if you've registered at jonathanwhistman.com/thesalesboss. This technique has the advantage of getting group participation and buy-in. It moves the discussion ahead to actionable items very quickly.

So now that we are clear that any meeting that doesn't have value is *changed and improved and not cancelled*, let's look at group meetings. It is important that you come up with a creative name for these meetings that describes the purpose. Perhaps use terms related to your industry. An airline-related company might use preflight, sorties, fly-ins, flight plan, chandelle, or others. If you aren't familiar with these flying terms, it's because you aren't in the industry. Remember that you increase the sense of belonging when you have a unique language. Use your unique names for these meetings and don't be boring.

# Group Meetings

## Weekly group check-in [You'll use another name]

This meeting should move quickly and needs to be highly structured. It is a quick state of the sales team meeting. I find it best to have these on Monday early or Friday morning. If you leave them until late on Friday, people won't be engaged and you'll get more absenteeism. This meeting has three parts.

During this first section the team members do an individual check-in with the group. They report their sale numbers or activity metrics for the period. They also give kudos to someone in the company and then say what their area of focus is in the next period. The check-ins proceed without any commentary from you. Don't let this ramble. In fact, with some of the best meetings I have seen, the check-in is scripted. If you script the check-in, it will set a rhythm and help people state clearly what is happening in their sales territory. Here is a sample script:

> "My sales for the year are _____ against the year's goal of _____. This last week I sold _____. I conducted _____ new prospecting visits and completed _____ executive overviews. That puts me ahead/behind where I need to be. Last week I committed to _____, and I was able to _____. Next week my specific focus is on _____. An area I could use some help on is _____. I'd like to give kudos to _____ for _____."

What happens when you start this way? It adds some peer pressure. Without saying a word, the individuals compare their behavior to the team's behavior. They will in many ways start to self-correct their behaviors. If they have a bad week, they'll work even harder to have a glowing check-in the following week. If the highest-selling person's activity numbers are higher than their own, they'll start to increase their activity. Nobody wants to be the person saying, "I completed five prospecting calls" when everyone else has been above fifteen.

This format also tells new hires that numbers and results are important and that they'd better know their numbers. It helps the "things are only good or bad by comparison" aspect of the team. It also allows you to change the script to include areas you feel are vital to the growth of the team's results. Choose a key metric to add to the check-in, and people's focus will shift to that item.

The second part of the meeting is yours. Share anything that impacts the team here: new promotions, upcoming trade shows, marketing changes, or anything that will equip them to do their jobs. Be positive and up-building. Give credit to the team. Restate who the enemy to sell against is if you have framed one for the team.

The last part of the meeting is for someone to share a win or a loss and what was learned so that the team can benefit. Assign this in advance to someone from something you have learned during the week's coaching sessions.

Of key importance: This meeting runs on time both beginning and end. It is never altered or canceled and people only miss it when they are on vacation. Nothing (not even a customer) is allowed to bump this meeting with your team. This is what I mean by Sacred Rhythms. This more rigid style of meeting is counterbalanced by the monthly meeting described next.

## Monthly roundtable [You'll use another name]

The tone of this meeting is relaxed and fun. This once-a-month meeting is where you do some deeper dive training or sharing of information. It is run in addition to the weekly check-in, not in replacement of one. You have a full month to plan this meeting, so it should never look thrown together. Use a theme or some other way of marking this as a well-prepared event. This meeting can be expanded to include people outside the actual sales team, but people whom the sales team needs to work with to do their best work. For instance, you might invite product managers, marketing, or quote writers to present to the group.

This meeting should start with a rhythm. For example, if your team has developed a certain way of introducing the company and folks are still learning it, you might start with someone role playing that intro. Keep doing this at the start of each roundtable until it has become second-nature and then substitute a new rhythm. I like to use a random assignment of who will do the role play; that way everyone reviews it in preparation for the meeting just in case he or she is chosen. Be careful not to pick on someone here. I avoid even the appearance of putting someone on the spot by having someone pick a name out of a hat. You can make this a fun part of the meeting and provide a learning lesson at the same time.

Use the remainder of the meeting for training and drills. The more often you drill, the more nimble your team will be when they are in front of a customer. It helps keep them in shape. You can also use this time to address key issues that affect the entire team or to plan for upcoming events such as tradeshows.

Give a monthly summary of results, then give some rewards and recognition. If possible, use a traveling trophy or something that creates a bit of humor and allows the person doing the rewarding to tell a story. Choose a story that tells a lesson. People remember good stories. Don't call to task an underperformer publicly. No benefit comes from it. On occasion a team scolding can be useful, but this is rare.

Have some fun as part of the meeting. Consider holding the meeting in different areas, in manufacturing or another department, at the local park or museum, or at one of your key vendor or customer locations. Avoid using your company's conference room every month. People will start to tune out and you'll have to work extra hard to get results if you do this meeting on autopilot. Use your imagination to create a great meeting. When people enter the room, have some upbeat music playing. If your meeting is a virtual meeting because your team is distributed in different physical locations, find an equivalent way to spice things up.

I find movie clips are a great way to make a point and add humor. For instance, I saw one manager use a YouTube video that was a remake of the scene from *A Few Good Men*. It was the scene when Tom Cruise cross-examines the general played by Jack Nicholson in a tense high-stakes courtroom scene. Tom needs to get Jack to admit to ordering the Code Red. In the end, Jack screams out in frustration and indignation, "You're Goddamn right I ordered the Code Red!" The clip was remade to be "A Few Good Expenses," and the point was about proper and improper expenses while traveling. It turns out the general was expensing lap dances, "You're Goddamn right I expensed the lap dance!" It was fun, humorous, and made the point.

The Sales Boss could have lectured for the hundredth time on controlling expenses, but instead he used his creativity to discuss an otherwise boring and sometimes emotional topic. TED Talks are also a great source for content to start or frame a meeting. If I were doing a meeting on sales leadership, I might select a clip from Derek Sivers, How to Start a Movement. Google and watch it.

I've seen other companies train with a full-stage mock-up of popular game shows complete with the Sales Boss dressed as Alex Trebek, Vanna White, or Oprah. Don't be too serious except when it comes to revenue results. If you need some help, get your marketing team or some interns involved in creating some cool meeting collateral.

This meeting is a prime time to be the thermostat and not the thermometer! You must set the temperature and energy level of the group. Do you need the team to believe, think, or feel a certain way? Then you must be there ahead of them. I remember someone early in my leadership career told me the story of the Dread Pirate Roberts, which has forever embedded in my mind the need for the leader to set the right tone.

Dread Pirate Roberts was feared on the high seas. He had a winning reputation and also some quirks of battle. Whenever he would spot a group of ships on the horizon, he would rally his band of pirates to ready for the fight, but would also say to his first mate: "Bring me my red pants!" The first mate would dutifully bring the red pants, and the battle would soon be won. After many successful battles, the first mate inquired of the captain: "Why do you always call for your red pants just before battle?" "That's simple," stated the captain, "I always call for my red pants so that if I am struck in battle by the enemy's sword and I bleed, the wound won't be visible to our fighters! We can't have them getting discouraged!"

This made sense to the first mate and he admired the bravery of Dread Pirate Roberts. A few days later, ships appeared on the horizon. This group of ships seemed much grander than their usual battles. All of a sudden Dread Pirate Roberts' voice rang out: "First mate, hurry to bring me my brown pants!"

This silly story has always served to remind me that when I am in front of my team, my demeanor has a substantial impact. I can choose what my team receives from me in terms of energy and enthusiasm. I can also choose the unwritten messages. Always be aware of your emotional state and the impact it will have on the team. Who you are *being* can be speaking so loudly that they won't hear what you are saying.

Your communication style says a lot about where you are coming from and what drives you. Are you leading from fear? Are you feeling the pressure of the sales target and upper management and allowing that to roll down on the team? Are you confident that your team is up to the challenge and will win? You've heard the old advertising slogan: "Never let them see you sweat." In the future ask yourself whether you have on your red pants or your brown ones.

## Yearly sales gathering [You will call it something else]

This gathering is what you might think of as the typical yearly sales meeting where new products are discussed, upcoming sales goals are announced, and there is some sort of awards event. Unlike the monthly meetings that may require not always being physically together as a team, the yearly meeting should always require everyone to be physically present.

These typically are several days long. These events must be well-devised and planned. Don't skimp on these events. Make sure the team comes away knowing the value you place on their participation in the success of the company. I find it helpful to bring in outside speakers when possible. There is the saying: "A prophet is never honored in his homeland." An outside voice is often heard more loudly than someone from within the company, just by nature of being from the outside. If you've followed the suggestions on great monthly meetings, you'll already have a high bar set for what people expect from a meeting, and you will need to raise the bar for this yearly event!

Allow some time outside of the meeting for the team to have natural moments to bond and interact with their fellow salespeople. This can be done at dinners, sports events, comedy shows (try improv where the salespeople can participate!), challenge courses, Go Kart tracks, hiking, and other activities. One company I know had sailing races with the teams each crewing a boat after a morning of practice and instruction. With a bit of creativity, they made the entire meeting themed around sailing to draw parallels between selling success and sailing success. The power and impact of the meeting came from the combination of increasing the sense of camaraderie and bonding among members of the team and anchoring that into a sensory experience relating to selling.

Don't schedule every minute full of meetings and presentations. If you've done the other meetings well throughout the year, this event becomes a very natural part of the year and one that the team enjoys. If geography and other circumstances permit, include a night when spouses and kids can be involved. In many sales jobs, the salesperson spends a lot of time away from the family traveling, so including family will be appreciated. There is also a benefit from seeing this facet of our teammates' lives. It gives everyone a more robust view of the team, resulting in closer and more authentic relationships.

Plan the meeting in such a way that your team will finish feeling a "good tired," not exhausted. They must walk out of the meeting with more energy than they had when they entered it only days previously. This is your opportunity to instill some of the company's traditions. If none existed when you came on board, now is the time to create some that will outlive your time as the Sales Boss.

# 13

# Individual Rhythms That Lead to Star Performances

# Individual Meetings Framework

Individual meetings are where you build relationships with your salespeople and customize the environment for growth. You must have some important one-on-one meetings with your salespeople, and this chapter outlines what should be accomplished at each one. Before we start looking at the tactical nature of what happens at these meetings, it is important to review your mindset and the "how you show up" at these meetings.

Remember the key points of the Management Code:

- Don't micro-manage; be actively engaged
- Honesty always; nobody should ever be surprised
- Be authentic; people are people
- Be the thermostat, not the thermometer
- Trust and expect the best, but verify
- Believe bigger
- Believe the fault is yours

Our meetings with our salespeople always come from this place. The best Sales Boss spends more than 80 percent of his or her time in the coaching and mentoring role and less than 20 percent in the boss and judge role. We will discuss each of these roles in detail.

Show up at individual meetings free of ego or predetermined judgments and with your highest EQ. Come to these meetings not to have your needs met, but to authentically help your salesperson. Recall that every salesperson is giving 100 percent of what he or she is capable of or has what he or she believes is a valid reason for not doing so. If you are unhappy with the results of a salesperson on your team, your job is to figure out what is going on.

A helpful framework for thinking about sales performance is using the term "boss" as an acronym: BOSS. I always say that a salesperson should sell like a "BOSS," meaning from a place of authority. The acronym encourages them to look at the levers that impact their ability to sell: Behavior, Outlook, Skills, and Stature. I have found it to be a great starting point for the Sales Boss to look at the performance of the individuals on the sales team. Really, there are just a few levers you can pull on the individual level that will impact sales results. BOSS captures these nicely.

## Behavior

Behavior deals with the quantity and habits that your salesperson has. How many calls, visits, contacts, make up the person's total activity? Behavior can include things like drinking, eating, and fitness. How organized is this person? Is he or she utilizing sales resources and tools? It is WHAT the person does, not HOW. Think of it this way: You could have someone who is a wizard at making cold calls and can get through to the decision-maker every time! The person has the perfect technique, but, if he never picks up the phone to dial or does so infrequently, then being a wizard at it has no material impact on the sales made. You need a balance between behavior and skill.

## Outlook

This is the area that has the biggest impact on results once you have a team of A-players. Outlook is how someone feels at any given moment. It changes. It could be outlook toward themselves, the marketplace, the economy, the competition, the company, toward you or any other person or thing. It might even include things happening outside of the workplace. Your one-on-one meetings will allow you to understand each person's outlook. Be observant as to which outlooks have changed or are in the process of changing. The language someone uses will give you clues as to the emotions being felt. When someone is feeling defeated, pressured, or angry, it is hard to turn in a winning performance. When one of your salespeople loses a deal that he worked hard on to a competitor, is he hanging onto the feeling of defeat? Blaming some other department for this result? "If only manufacturing could have delivered in a more competitive timeline!" Stay in tune with the changing outlook of your team members and you'll be ahead of many sales performance issues.

## Skills

This is the HOW they do it, not WHAT they do. How do they introduce the company? What types of questions do they ask prospects? What about their body language and tone of voice? This is the skills development area. One salesperson could make double the number of visits as another salesperson on the team, but if she lacks the right techniques she will still suffer from poor results. People can be working hard, but not effectively.

## Stature

This phrase is meant to capture the "essence" of how people are viewed by others. Do they have the weight of a consultant and the demeanor of a trusted advisor? Their look, their tone, their vibe, their online presence, or anything that changes the way they are viewed by a prospect can impact this essence.

# Three Types of Individual Meetings

Let's discuss three types of meetings: pipeline performance review, skills and process coaching, and the sales ride-along. As with all meetings and rhythms, name these meetings in a way that is unique to your team rather than use generic labels.

## Pipeline performance review

This meeting happens monthly. It brings more of the boss and judge role to the table, rather than the coach and mentor, although you'll include a blend of all. During this meeting, you will discuss any key performance measures, such as prospecting expectations, CRM usage, outstanding quotes, changes in outcomes that were previously forecast, etc. Look at the top deals in the pipeline and have a deeper discussion about what is happening. Take some notes. From month to month, you'll start to know when things change related to an opportunity. Last month the salesperson spoke excitedly about an opportunity, but now seems reticent. What has happened? Only by taking good notes will you remember what was said in the past, and taking notes honors the person by letting him or her know you think it is important. Again, I recommend using Evernote if you don't currently have another system in place for tracking your notes. What stands in the way of closing these deals? How can you help? What resources are needed?

Discuss sales quotas and targets. Do they have enough in their pipelines to reach their targets? If not, what actions must they take? Are they using your company's CRM and other systems as required? Although you might accomplish some "light coaching" during this session, it is more likely that you will take note of needed training and provide that training at another time. During this meeting, you focus on the numbers. Again, with results comes less scrutiny. Dig deeper with folks who are struggling. Question the legitimacy of the numbers harder.

Be sure to ask how they feel about their results and what they believe must be done. Get them to make commitments. You will "encourage the heart," as described by Jim Kouzes and Barry Posner in *The Leadership Challenge*, but kick their butts as needed. They should not be looking forward to meeting if they have been consistently underperforming, but if it's just a recent slump they should be confident that this meeting will help them sort it out.

An important portion of this meeting is to talk about upcoming meetings with prospects. You should ask whether the visits are on the schedule, what their approach will be, and the outcome they expect. Again, take notes with Evernote. Follow up at your next meeting. It is through these discussions that you will get a feel for how "real" things are, plus how your salespeople think and plan their prospecting visits. You might role play some of the calls ahead of time or help them identify internal and external resources that could be helpful as they prepare for the visits. Many of your coaching discussions can come from the difference between what the salesperson thought would happen and what actually happened.

The salesperson's forecasts come from this pipeline meeting, so the importance of accuracy needs to be stressed. If you are hearing wishy-washy answers or the person is continuing to have issues that are not resolving despite your help and coaching, then this is the meeting where pressure should be increased. If underperformers push back, it's OK to remind them that they weren't doing so hot before they came into your office. You are going to call their fluffiness (B.S.) by looking at the numbers for phone calls, emails, travel expenses, and pipeline.

An increasing level of pressure might sound like this:

"Steve, the last few meetings we've been talking about the need for you to increase the number of prospecting visits made each week in order for you to have enough in your pipeline to meet your goal. This is a solution you suggested yourself.

"Last time you thought it would be reasonable for you to increase that number to X. It looks like you didn't reach that number again. This isn't like you. Normally, you deliver on what you say you will do. What happened? _____ What do you think the solution might be? _____ OK, let's do that.

"Let me ask you, if we are here again next month after you make this commitment, and we are having this same discussion about you failing to do what you commit to, what do you think I should do? _____ How long would you allow this problem to go on without being taken seriously if you were responsible for the sales team? _____ I'm taking this seriously, Steve, because the company counts on us to deliver. Even more importantly, I know you set an earnings goal for yourself. How will failing to hit your money goal affect you? I remember you mentioned _____ "

When salespeople do not take corrective action, it is usually because there were never clear conversations about what action should be taken and the salesperson was not involved in the solution. Get people to commit to the solution or even argue with you that it isn't a problem. The worst thing is for there to be an issue nobody is talking about. Be the Sales Boss and sit in judgment. There should be no ambiguity about performance.

Once you are done with each very thorough pipeline meeting, resist the urge to ask about the forecast for the rest of the month. Don't ask for another update unless something critical demands it. Trust your team to deliver what they said. If they fail, this is the meeting to address it. Too many sales managers get micro-focused on updates to the forecast, which actually inhibits the work of selling. You should not be calling for updates repeatedly throughout the month, as this will be seen as micromanaging—and it will have little impact anyhow.

When your efforts are focused on behaviors, outlook, skills, and stature, the numbers will take care of themselves. Don't think you can run the team from the viewport of the CRM. I see plenty of sales managers who are addicted to the CRM. If you want to be the Sales Boss, use the CRM only when you need it. Then put it away to go out and get dirty with the actual work of coaching, training, motivating, adjusting, and inspiring others on your team. For most size teams, I would spend less than 45 minutes in the CRM per day. If you get buried in emails, nonmeetings, putting out fires, and approving expense reports, then it is your fault. I've heard these referred to as "Time Draculas," as in "I want to suck your time!" The more busywork and administration work you do, the more confined your results will be.

## Skills and process coaching

In addition to the skills training that is offered to the group, it is important that you have ongoing coaching on a one-to-one basis. These more intimate conversations will allow you to understand what is going on with your salespeople individually. Spend some time before your meetings reflecting on the behavior, outlook, skills, and stature of the salesperson to plan in advance an area that you want to focus on. Start with any area that is identified by the salesperson as a need, but always have something to fall back on in case the salesperson indicates everything is fine. During this meeting you can assess the knowledge level of the salesperson to track where he or she should be relevant to time with your company.

If you want to be a real master at the coaching aspect of your role as Sales Boss, be prepared to be "present." This means that when you are one-on-one with a salesperson, you are fully with the person and not still thinking about your last meeting, checking emails, or otherwise sending the message that you are busy or multi-tasking. It is often between the lines of the conversation that you will discover the real truth, and in order to read between the lines you'll need to be fully present. Start preparing before the appointed meeting time to clear your mind. Breathe deeply and contemplate the impact you'd like to have in the coaching sessions and then show up fully present.

Use role playing during your coaching. You will find that most people hate doing role play; however, it is one of the most effective ways to practice techniques. You can take the pressure off by acknowledging that role play isn't 100 percent real, but that some truths come out in role play. If you are playing the prospect role, resist the temptation to play "gotcha." Use role-play scenarios that come up frequently, and not the weird things that happen once in 1,000 calls. Make sure that you record these role plays, since seeing and hearing themselves will allow salespeople to grow in ways that won't happen otherwise.

One of the things you will notice in a sales team that role plays frequently is that they have a high degree of mental flexibility. They increase the range of responses that are available to them when they are in the selling situation. Have you ever been on a sales call and later think: "I wish I would have said X . . . or done Y." This is an indication of not being mentally flexible. It took you too long to realize the position you needed to be in with the prospect. The goal is to think of what you wish to do or say while you are still in front of the prospect and can do something about it. When you role play with your team, you will see this happen more frequently and they will get better at it over time. A few areas ripe for role play include:

- The first five minutes of a sales call
- Questioning skills

- Overcoming stalls and objections
- Prospecting phone calls
- Presentation skills
- Quote reviews
- Qualifying skills
- Negotiation

Develop a list of what behavior, outlook, skills, and stature you want your salespeople to have. Make a written list and grade each area as you have your coaching sessions. You might not show a salesperson the grading list, but it will serve to keep your coaching on target.

A word of warning: After you have held role-play sessions for months, it will be tempting to stop doing them, as some of the practice will become repetitive. Don't give in to this temptation. Think of these sessions as drills. If you were the coach of a sports team, you would continue to run the same basic drills no matter how talented the people on the team were. Athletes can always get faster and stronger and commit key movements to muscle memory. You want the same from your selling team. Your future success is locked up in these coaching sessions. Pipeline reviews are almost always looking back or predicting the next quarter of customer behavior and buying. Coaching is removed from this aspect and serves to equip your salespeople for a lifetime of selling success. It keeps them healthy and in competitive shape.

You can't transform your company through coaching alone. You must connect the coaching to performance. The reality I see is that salespeople are not raising their game as quickly as buyers are raising theirs. Consequently, they show up late in the buying cycle, need to play catch up, discount pricing, and fail to establish themselves as trusted advisors to the buyers. Are your salespeople capable of making the kind of sales call that the prospect would willingly write a check for? Do they bring that much value on the sales call or only get paid when the product and service are delivered?

These coaching sessions are not the time for the questions I hear inexperienced sales managers ask: "Are you hitting your numbers?" "How many calls did you make?" "Are you following up?" "How many appointments did you schedule?" Those questions will surface at times in your pipeline meetings, but will only be asked if your coaching goal directly links to one of these questions. You'll more often hear questions such as: "What did you do well?" "What's the lesson here?" "What was the result you were looking for when you took that approach?" "How can I help you handle this better next time?" "What do you feel should change?" "What resources could have an impact?" "Where is the opportunity?" "How do you think this mindset is impacting your results?" "How are you feeling?" "What has your energy level been like lately?" "If that happens, then what?" "Why that way?" "What would you like to be doing that you aren't already?" "What does success look like here?" "Looking forward, how do you see. . . ?"

When you are coaching, state things from the positive side when possible. Only use fear and authority sparingly. Note these two approaches to the same problem:

> "If you keep being disorganized, your stress level is just going to increase and eventually this whole thing becomes an unmanageable mess. I don't know why you don't get organized. I hope I don't have to bring this up again."

versus

> "If you follow through on some of the daily routines we've discussed, I think you'll find your stress level goes

down and you'll continue to achieve at higher levels without being overwhelmed. I think you might even start enjoying your job again. Let's do what we've discussed and next time we get together you tell me if it is helping. Fair?"

Choose your words and approach carefully. You need your salespeople to have confidence, and confidence comes from competence. Competence comes from training and experience. Make sure that your salespeople are learning from their experiences. I've met people who have been in sales for fifteen years or more. When I've done a sales ride-along it would be tough to know that they've had more than a couple of years of experience. Does your salesperson have fifteen years of experience or one year of experience repeated fifteen times? If you don't keep the conversation focused on incremental improvements, your salespeople will plateau at the moment they start having some moderate levels of success. They'll stop stretching themselves to be better. Your goal is to provide the environment and expectation for ongoing growth.

During these one-on-one coaching sessions, you should be developing a good understanding of the goals and motivations of your salespeople. You'll also discover how they define what success and greatness are. The real magic in these sessions will happen when you find effective ways to expand their views of what is possible.

What words typically define a coaching relationship? Here are a few. As you read the list, think back to the sessions you have with your salespeople. Are you accessing the entire range of coaching?

- Advising
- Agreeing

- Asking
- Correcting
- Deliberating
- Directing
- Discussing
- Expressing
- Guiding
- Inspiring
- Instructing
- Leading
- Listening
- Nudging
- Probing
- Reflecting
- Teaching
- Telling

While this isn't an exhaustive list, it should help you to appreciate that you have a wide range of options when considering how to interact with someone. Choose the method that is most likely to achieve results. We tend to approach coaching in the way that is most comfortable for us, when in reality we should be asking ourselves: "What is the most effective way for achieving the desired change in the person being coached?"

An effective coach is free of the need to look right, be looked up to, or prove a point. When you are having a session with a salesperson and find yourself feeling there is a struggle for power or a tug of war, then you need to step back and make sure your ego isn't involved.

A phrase sometimes used in communications classes is "always already listening." It refers to our predisposition to view something a certain way, thus affecting what we hear or perceive in the communication. As an example, you might think "I hate classical music." How would this affect your ability to judge a piece of classical music? At the very least you would have that voice in your head and be rolling your eyes as you heard the first few notes. You would expect to hate it. Someone else might listen expecting to love it.

Think of the impact that "always already listening" might have on our coaching if we have already decided the salesperson won't change, isn't up to the task, or whatever. Or perhaps we have a strong bias that a certain way of doing something is always correct, so it closes us off to hearing and exploring new ways to do things. This type of thinking can hinder your flexibility and adaptability and, thus, your impact as a coach. Practice asking yourself: "Do I have evidence to support my opinions and assumptions or how I am feeling?" You might also ask yourself: "If what I am thinking/feeling about this situation was not true, what might an alternate explanation be?" The key is to make sure our own biases aren't causing distortions in how we approach our coaching.

Don't fall in love with your own voice. Make sure that you are listening to your salesperson and that you are testing out what you hear to make sure you understand the person correctly. People desire to be heard. A technique from the world of coaching can help you. It is a combination of reflective listening (where you repeat what has just been said) and clarifying. Here are some examples:

- For my own understanding . . .
- What you are truly saying is . . .
- What I just heard is . . .
- Help me to understand further . . .
- Can you tell me a bit more about that?
- It sounds like the criteria you are using to make a decision are . . .

- What do you mean?
- Can you rephrase that so I better understand?

Each of these phrases, when combined with authenticity and curiosity, will help you to have clear communication and a bond with the person you are coaching.

It's essential to know when enough is enough. People can and will only change so much over a given period. You must be patient and realize that change will happen incrementally and that it is simply a part of an ongoing process. If you need massive changes from a salesperson, it is quite likely you have the wrong person on your team. Remember, the cats shouldn't be on your team. This coaching time is planned, not handed out to the squeakiest wheel.

Video-record some of your sales meetings and coaching sessions. Just like recording your salespeople's role play helps them to improve, seeing your own demeanor will help you identify areas for improvement. I seriously recommend reading as many books dealing with coaching as you can, and take a class on effective coaching. Better yet, hire a coach so you can experience what great coaching is. This is the skill that all of your other successes as a Sales Boss will hinge around. Above all, learning about coaching will help you to realize that real coaching isn't about "fixing" something. Sometimes, you simply need to hear a person out and help reflect back his or her thinking and choices so the best path forward becomes clear. This view of coaching doesn't require you always to be jumping in with a solution. Yes, there is a time to have a solution or help fix the salesperson's problem. It just doesn't have to be every time. Your role sometimes is simply to be impressed with your salesperson and to believe great things are possible.

Let's face it though, sometimes you have to be the bearer of bad news. Sometimes you have to be the tough guy. One technique for delivering bad news is to trade a bit on the relationship, share respect that you have between yourself and the salesperson, then "ask for permission" to deliver the news. This simple technique can lesson the person's defensive instinct and take a bit of the bite out without diminishing the strength of your message. Here's how that might sound:

> "Can I point something out that might be tough for you to hear right now?"
>
> "I have something I need to share with you, but I am afraid it might sting just a bit. I'm sharing it, as I know it will be for your good. I just need to know you are open to hearing it. OK?"
>
> "You might not like what I am about to say, but my role is to speak the truth about what I see from my point of view. Can I share with you something you might be uncomfortable hearing but that I think is limiting you right now?"
>
> "If you want help on this, I need you to tell me you'll be OK hearing some tough feedback. Fair?"
>
> "I know you are capable of more. Would it be OK if I just lay things on the line with you? I sincerely believe if you can take a look at this without getting upset that it would help your success."

These types of softening statements allow people to emotionally prepare for what is coming next and lessen the likelihood that they'll have a sharp reaction that they later regret.

Make time during your coaching sessions for *involved recognition*, which means that you don't just say, "Good job." It means you are specific about what was done, how it was done, and the results it had on the client or company. It might sound like:

> "I was really impressed with the way you handled ABC Company. Your persistence in getting in and understanding

the key players helped position us to win the deal. When you were able to call their CFO directly and gain some insight into the process, it paid off. We couldn't have won the new business without that. You should feel proud of your accomplishment!"

Avoid following involved recognition with any statement that starts with "But. . . ." Allow people time to bask in the recognition. A pro tip is to write out the involved recognition and mail it to people's homes after you've praised them. It allows them to brag a bit to a spouse, who may wonder from whom the nice card arrived today.

"Oh, it's nothing. The Sales Boss just thinks I really made a difference in getting a nice piece of business for the company."

People might tell you they don't need that kind of recognition, and some don't. But everyone loves receiving it, even if they don't need it. You will see the behaviors you praised repeated more often.

You should also give opportunities for your superstars to take on new challenges and have a wider degree of impact. For instance, you might ask them to plan trade-show events; help in launching or testing a new product; or serve on an industry panel or trade group board. You can talk about these enhanced opportunities during your sessions. One of the key drivers in keeping superstars happy is to honor their need to feel like they are still growing and learning. Provide as many of these opportunities as possible while not distracting them from their selling responsibilities. These additional activities should be directly related to growing their sales in some capacity.

While these coaching sessions might be less formal than the pipeline reviews, you should still follow a general agenda so the time is not wasted. Most coaching sessions will grow organically and take on a shape of their own, which is good, but you will also want enough structure to assure an outcome. A typical session follows this general format:

- Small talk/emotional check in
- Agree to expectations for the time
- Check in on past action items
- Coaching conversation (may be specific issue or more free-form discovery)
- Connect to results
- Commitment to any action steps
- Summarize and check acceptance/attitude
- Conclude by reconfirming next meeting

Don't get stuck on the agenda format, but make sure that your time has had value and purpose. This isn't just a chat.

In addition to coaching sessions, you will want to include some joint sales calls, sometimes called ride-alongs if they are happening out in the field. Keep all of the coaching strategies we've just discussed in mind and use them while in the field.

## Effective ride-alongs

As the Sales Boss, you are almost always in the mode of wanting your team to close the sale. This mindset can hinder you when you are out in the field with your salesperson. It is all too easy to and jump in to rescue people when they face what appears to be a problem. While this may seem to be helpful, it does not accomplish what a sales ride-along should. For these ride-alongs to have real value, you must be willing to detach yourself from the outcome of the call and focus strictly on providing the training and feedback that will equip your salesperson to become better, even if that means losing this sale. You don't need to be the hero. Sometimes the best learning comes from failing. Be willing to let people fail.

Your observational radar must be fully engaged when in the field. Don't spend time looking at your phone answering emails and otherwise be distracted. Be fully focused on the person you are with: How does the person look, sound, interact with, and react to the prospect? What techniques does she utilize? How authentic does he seem? Is she well prepared and organized? Does he use good questions? What stories does she tell to illustrate her ideas? You can find a sample of a ride-along evaluation form using the online resource page at www.jonathanwhistman/thesalesboss.

There are a few different types of ride-alongs, and you will want to discuss ahead of time what type a particular sales call will be so everyone understands the role he or she will be playing on the call. You might have a learning ride, a silent observer, a tag team, or an unannounced ride-along.

**Learning ride**   In this case, the salesperson is in the observer role, and you conduct the entire call. This can be helpful when someone is new to the company or your team. It is also effective when the salesperson must overcome a habit that is impacting his or her success, but is having difficulty understanding the impact a change would have. For instance, I teach salespeople a very structured start to a call that encourages the prospect to share early in the call. Sometimes salespeople need to see this approach in action and the dramatic difference in results from prospects before they are comfortable adopting the approach. When done in role play, they can't get over feeling as though the approach is canned, but seeing it in action they clearly see the magic in the approach and how natural it can sound.

For this type of call to be successful, you should clearly state before the call why you are conducting it and the skill or technique that you want the salesperson to observe. After the call, you will want to debrief the person's observations. For instance, you might say, "Steve, we have focused in our training on the need to probe deeper with our prospects before prescribing a solution. One of the ways we do this is by asking a series of questions before providing an answer. On this call, I'd like you to observe what questions seem to have the most impact on getting the prospect to tell us the real issue. Make a mental note also of additional questions you think I should have asked but didn't." Notice how specific this directive is. It is not a generalized "Watch me and learn!"

I remember one particular salesperson who struggled with setting up an appropriate frame for the sales call and who often ended up in late-stage negotiating against a competitor who had lower prices. In training sessions we discussed the tactic of bringing up the price difference right from the beginning. Although the salesperson could intellectualize the concept, each time we were in the field he would fail to execute the sales strategy out of fear that it was the wrong time and would set a poor tone with the customer. Unless I could get him past that mental block, he would never try the new strategy.

We must remember that whatever fears people have are based on their experiences, and that fear is neither good nor bad, but simply information that we can use when coaching them. Many times the fear is self-reinforcing, as they act in a way that is congruent with their beliefs about how the customer will react. Sometimes a learning ride is the best option to remove the fear and move the skill level forward. With this in mind, I offered to lead the next sales call where we knew that we would be up against the lower-priced competitor. After a brief introduction, I said, "Tom, based on what you've shared with us so far and the type of solutions that are typically called on in this scenario, I can predict that our quote will come in at least 30 percent more than the other company's. I know we have a lot more work to do before knowing whether we are the right fit, but could you ever see a situation where you'd pay 30 percent more?" I could sense the salesperson tense up as he watched me. The prospect said, "That's a pretty steep difference! I guess there would have to be a pretty big reason." I followed with: "In your experience, Tom, why do you think our customers choose to spend 30 percent more with us when they could go to our competition for less?" He responded, "Well, I suppose the quality. Things that are cheap to start with always have trouble. In fact, I remember an installation where we had so much trouble we ended up paying more than what we would have paid going with the highest bid." We talked specifics about that story and then drilled into what he would need to know in order to choose us as the higher-priced option. We won the business. The salesperson's fear was lessened, and now he leads every call with a discussion about the price. All it took was for him to see an example outside of the classroom setting. This is the purpose of the learning ride.

**Silent observer**    On this call your goal is to participate as little as possible. You still need the call to seem natural and to have a total mute on the call isn't natural, but you will intentionally limit your impact on the direction of the call. You will simply observe, with the idea of being able to provide feedback. For this type of call, you must resist the desire to interject and influence the flow of the call. In these moments as a silent observer you will be able to see how your salesperson thinks about the sales process and how that shows up in the field. Once again, if you are working on a specific skill, you will want to state that prior to the call and debrief afterward.

You can go back to the list of training topics, and all of these are potential areas to focus on during the ride-along. You must be specific in your feedback and cite real examples of what happened on the call. Be comfortable giving a critique. You might also probe for understanding by asking why the salesperson chose to present something a certain way or ask a certain series of questions. These learning insights will help you coach. I use the example with salespeople I travel with of sitting down to a Thanksgiving meal and being asked to critique the meal. Sometimes everything tastes delicious, and if I had preferred a bit more of this or that spice it doesn't mean it was a poor meal. So it is when I critique the sales call. It doesn't mean it was bad; it is just an opinion of how things might be spiced differently. You should start with the assumption that the sales call is done well and, even if it is perfect, you will have two or three observations of areas for improvement. Your best salespeople will value feedback.

As an example, one salesperson I rode with easily develops relationships and closes business as a result. During one particular call, however, I noticed that early in the initial discussion he offered to create sample packages for the prospect, a process that would take weeks. Once he made the offer, the prospect agreed and the call quickly ended with details on shipping product to the manufacturer being arranged so samples could be created. The salesperson will close this business; however, he unnecessarily extended the selling cycle by offering something that was not requested and without gaining any commitment from the prospect in return. After the call we were able to walk through a list of "unknowns" that could have been "knowns" if the salesperson had continued to ask questions rather than jumping to an early solution. While not deadly, this small change has allowed the salesperson to close deals more quickly without adding to the overhead cost to his company by offering to do samples as a means of moving the process forward. Now he only offers this if it is requested and doing so serves a key purpose, and if he gets some agreements in advance as to next steps. This is the type of refinement your team will achieve as you observe actual calls. I would not have discovered this issue in training sessions alone.

I observed that another salesperson would treat the receptionist coldly, and after giving her his card and asking to see the prospect, he would sit quietly in the reception room without engaging in any small talk. After the call we discussed what value there would be in gaining insight about the company and the prospect by chatting with the receptionist. On future calls, as he made an effort to be friendly, he started gaining an advantage as he created an ally with the receptionist. I share these examples to show how seemingly small observations can impact results when you are present in the field with your team.

Another key benefit of rides-alongs is that you learn and discover what works with your prospects as you observe some of the best people. You are then in a position to share best practices with the rest of the team.

**Tag team**   On this ride-along you are both fully participating in the call. Typically, you will see this method used when the deal is critical and the purpose of the ride-along is to provide further resources to help win the deal. In this scenario you aren't there to teach the salesperson anything but are there to use your leverage and authority as the Sales Boss to close the business. Sometimes this can come at a key negotiating stage and holds value when the customer appreciates getting some additional attention by having the Boss available.

**Unannounced**   Usually you will have planned trips with your salespeople. Occasionally, however, you may want to make last-minute arrangements to accompany someone on sales calls. This is, of course, dependent on your type of business and the location of the team, but you might call one of your team members late in the day and say something like: "I had an appointment cancel on me and have a hole in my schedule tomorrow and would love to ride with you. Where should I meet you and at what time?" The key is to give as little notice as practical.

What you will experience on these ride-alongs is usually a truer picture of a typical day in the life of your salesperson. Fewer visits, fewer calls, and more interruptions are likely. If the salesperson says he or she can't do a ride-along on short notice, then your radar should go on full alert. The goal in these unannounced visits is simply to see what is real and authentic rather than what can sometimes be a prettier version when the person had plenty of notice.

After making a call to a salesperson and letting him know I'd be riding with him the next day, I was told we'd be working the territory nearest his home. He met me at the airport and we headed out to see a client who had recently purchased a large piece of equipment from the company with the stated goal of checking in to see how things were going. When we arrived, the plant manager, who was anxious to show us into the building where the machine was located, met us at the gate. It turned out that the machine had been having problems all week and the salesperson's company had a technician on-site. The salesperson was surprised, even though his company kept a log of where each technician was for the day. Clearly, he wasn't doing any pre-call planning. If this was the case for customers, I had to believe it was even worse for prospects. Time would prove me correct.

Later in the day, the salesperson said we would swing by a prospective company he'd been trying to connect with. I asked him to give me the background, as this target company was a major player and close to his home base. He stated that he'd been playing phone tag for months to no avail. We pulled up to the gate and the salesperson asked to see the contact. The guard at the gate indicated that, without an appointment, we couldn't be seen. The salesperson pulled his car out of the drive, giving up hope about seeing the prospect. I suggested we call and see whether the person was in and available since we were so close. The salesperson pulled out his CRM and after ten minutes of hunting and pecking dialed a number. It was the wrong number. Nowhere did he have an accurate phone contact number. It was clear that he had not been reaching out to this prospect for months. It was also obvious that it had been a long time since he'd been in the CRM. I used my phone, asking Siri for the number. I had it in seconds and dialed the number. I asked the receptionist to be put through to the contact. The receptionist stated that the person no longer worked at the company and had left six months previously.

I had uncovered the truth. This salesperson was clearly not working effectively, if he was working at all. I hope when you do an unannounced ride-along you won't experience disasters such as the one I described, but you will uncover behavior that is closer to the truth. The sales team that knows you might appear for a ride-along at any time tends to stay more disciplined. I've heard sales managers say, "Well, if that's the type of person he is I wouldn't want him on the team. I hire professionals and expect they'll act like adults. I shouldn't have to babysit them."

I agree. The only problem is that, even with professionals, you have to babysit just a bit. It is human nature to go on auto-pilot and to get comfortable. This isn't just true on the sales level. Think of the preparation, energy, and effort of the executive team when they are preparing for a presentation to the board of directors. Usually you'll notice a sharp uptick in attention to detail. This isn't because they aren't professionals. It's because they are now off autopilot and engaged in the work at hand. Your salespeople will react in a similar way when you travel with them.

As a general rule, I find that the best improvements come when the Sales Boss can do a minimum of two silent observer rides a year with the top performer. Of course, new and up-and-coming stars might have monthly or quarterly ride-alongs. If possible, you should be out as often as you can without overwhelming the team. An average of two or three days a week on ride-alongs or 100-plus days a year is not unusual for a Sales Boss. There is never a level of selling success at which you don't arrange a ride-along with a salesperson at some point in the year. If your team is so large that riding along with everyone is impossible, then you might consider hiring an outside consultant to do some ride-alongs. Your team will never reach the highest level of performance without these live calls.

If important parts of the selling process are conducted over the phone, you should also find a way to observe calls and give feedback. You might consider having some of the calls recorded so that you can analyze them with the salesperson after the fact.

One of the things you will notice when you offer training is that many of your team will say, "Oh yes, I do that!" But in reality they don't. Attending real sales calls with your team allows you to say, "This is what you actually do. . . ." This clarity between what they think they do and what actually happens is what helps you to coach for results. Regular role plays after live ride-alongs start to create confidence and mental flexibility in your sales team. They start to think more quickly and respond more accurately when in front of the customer.

So far we have talked about formal meetings, your meetings with the entire group, and your one-on-one meetings. In addition to these planned meetings, you should arrange in your week a time for an informal check-in via phone. This isn't pre-planned, but it lets the salespeople know you are thinking about them. It might be as simple as "Hey, I know you had that important call you were looking forward to with Mr. Smith. I'd love to hear how you felt it went!" or "I hope your flight went without too many challenges." "What new conversations are you most excited about?" "I saw you had a demo scheduled with X. What do they do?" These informal "taps on the shoulder" will let you be engaged and take the temperature of your team without micro-managing.

Once you have these regular meetings on your schedule, you should be able to avoid the "have-a-minute?" meetings. You know, those so-called quick stops by your office door with someone asking whether you have a minute that end up eating up all of your time. You can reduce these by helping people to think, plan, and prepare for your scheduled meetings. When you first implement your rhythm of meetings, you will have some people who don't come prepared to discuss their prospects and selling challenges, then later that same day bombard you with questions. This is a good time to remind them that these are the perfect types of questions to ask during your team or individual meetings. As you continue to progress, get in the habit of asking them whether an issue is something that could wait until your scheduled meeting. Of course, there will always be last-minute things that require an immediate answer, and you don't want to stifle conversations. Just make sure you are aware of your time. Train your people to see the benefit of asking questions and discussing issues at your meetings, where they have your full undivided attention and you are prepared to take notes to follow up on critical items discussed.

When you bring attention and focus to one-to-one conversations with each of your team members, you will experience a level of loyalty, devotion, and results that is simply not achieved by a traditional sales manager. As the Sales Boss, you will have a team that is excited and motivated to continue growing beyond what they believed they were capable of. They will be proud to work alongside you.

# Keep Score Publicly; Motivate Individually

Once you understand your sales process and the key metrics that drive selling success, you should have the foundation for keeping score. Scores should be posted publicly. If you are using your CRM tool effectively, it is simple to have a visual dashboard that shows each of the key metrics in easy-to-understand graphs. These dashboards should be seen not only when people log into the CRM, but also on a large-screen TV in the office that publicly displays these real-time results. The results should be individualized so people can see how they relate to the rest of the team. By doing this, you are leveraging the human behavior tendencies we discussed earlier: People want to belong, and things are good or bad by comparison.

If someone is having a bad month and is fourth on the list for dollars sold, he or she will think: "I might be bad, but I'm not that bad!" And he or she will work extra hard to rise on the list.

Don't list just the sales totals. List all of the metrics that are relevant to your team. Some companies list total prospecting calls, live demos, lost accounts, total quote volume, win/loss percentages, and margins. You are trying to tell a story of what is important through the data that is displayed. Beware of the unintended consequences that arbitrary numbers can have. For instance, if there is a focus strictly on the number of quotes issued, you might find salespeople indiscriminately sending out quotes to unqualified prospects, creating more follow-up and support work for the rest of the team than is required. Make your scorecard balanced in a way that tells an accurate story, and then coach for accuracy from your team. This combination will produce good and accurate results. The biggest metric at the end of the day should be money in the door. More than any other role, selling is results-based.

While we post results publicly, it is almost never appropriate to publicly talk about low performance from an individual. Simply having results posted is enough. When you are discussing the results as a group, focus on the individual positives and the group improvements that are necessary. When you must talk specifically about an individual who is doing poorly, try to do so in private. This is a balance between posting publicly and respecting the feelings of each person on the team. We don't hide poor performance, but we don't do public beatings. One of the advantages of publicly posting results is that the team's competitive nature will supply a natural motivational pressure that will improve results, so you won't need to create that pressure arbitrarily.

A powerful way to use the visual dashboard during meetings is to hold your meetings with the dashboard visible. You can teach your team how to think about the dashboard results by your skillful use of questions: What does the trend in outgoing quotes likely mean for our results next quarter? What is the correlation between the increase of new business and the decrease in prospecting activity telling us? What should we be focused on if we want to sustain the success we are having? Based on the numbers, what activities should be most critical for us to focus on this week?

The Sales Boss embraces metrics and uses the results to teach, coach, and diagnose but then gets to the heart of what the metrics are telling him about his market and the people on his team. It is much like a doctor who uses blood tests to indicate where to look for the cause of disease. In the end, what is done with those results in creating a treatment plan and executing the plan for the health of the patient has real meaning. By themselves, blood test results are meaningless. Make sure that the data you post publicly has a reason for existing. One of the ancillary benefits of posting results publicly is that it starts to thicken the skin of your sales team and they become more comfortable discussing their results and the results of the team. This approach also reduces the need for you to bring their standing to their attention. They'll see their results each day.

Although you will keep score publicly, you must also remember that people are motivated by different things and so will require different approaches to keep them operating at a high level. The posting of results is not primarily for motivation; it is for accountability and to leverage group dynamics and human nature to produce changes in thought and behavior. You can't mass produce motivation. It happens at the individual level. Salespeople tend to be competitive by nature, and you'll certainly leverage that. But high achievers also like to compete with themselves by beating their own numbers. Others pride themselves on continual learning or acquiring new experiences. If you have a personal relationship with members of your team, you can design plans for helping to motivate them. We've talked about people's need to belong and also about how they develop their views of what "great" is. Your job as the Sales Boss is to understand what drives each person. This isn't necessarily rational or something the salesperson can tell you. You can discover people's motivation by keen observation and personal conversation.

I remember traveling with a sales guy and hearing him talk about his hobbies. He recounted having competed in dog shows and the joy he received from his dog receiving best in class or other awards. Later, as we continued to talk, I discovered that he also collected cars and enjoyed entering them in car shows on the weekends. What did these insights help me to understand about his motivation? He had a deep-seated need for recognition. He desired to be recognized as the best. If you asked him directly, he might downplay this need, but his hobbies revealed the motivation. His Sales Boss would be wise to offer public symbols that recognize high achievement. This could be in the form a trophy, an expensive watch, or signature clothing only given to top achievers. Offering concrete items that the salesperson could point to with pride and recount the story of winning would provide ongoing motivation. Can you visualize the sales guy in his living room pointing out to guests the ribbon won at a dog or car show? Can you see the grin on his face and the emotion with which he tells the story? If so, figure out a way to re-create that experience when he has sales success and you'll have figured out how to keep a good level of motivation. People work hard to satisfy needs, whether emotional, physical, or psychological. Needs create an unexpressed tension. A salesperson will work to relieve that tension by moving toward something that fulfills those needs.

Another salesperson I traveled with had a picture of his kids tucked into the crease of his writing tablet. When we ate dinner, his stories centered on the activities that his kids were involved in. He spoke of coaching their sports teams, and I could see the pride he had in recounting the moments when something new "clicked" for his kids and they were able to achieve something for the first time. Later, as we traveled, he revealed that he also volunteered as a church mentor and would work with couples who were struggling in their marriages. What did these stories reveal to me about his motivation? What action should his Sales Boss have taken as a result? Clearly, this person's motivation centered on teaching and caretaking, and a wise Sales Boss would try to re-create this experience as part of his job role. One of the ways that this could be accomplished is by asking the salesperson to teach newer sales reps or to participate in leading some of the sales meetings.

You might also add to people's motivation by working the language of helping into your coaching sessions. This might sound like: "Joe, I know the team really looks up to the example you set when it comes to developing strong relationships with your clients. Maybe at our next meeting you would be willing to talk about the sales process you went through with XYZ customer, especially as it relates to how you developed your rapport with each of the stakeholders." A conversation like this will feed the need for significance and impact that is the driving motivational force for the salesperson.

When thinking about what motivates people, it is helpful to listen to what fills them with pride or what perks up the energy level when they speak. It is not unusual to find people motivated by quality of life or leisure time, recognition, trust, prestige, security or more flexibility, challenge and achievement, sense of belonging, authority, self-esteem, feelings of usefulness or progress, compensation, or promotions. These are all external factors that help influence internal motivation. By themselves, none of these might seem important, but when paired with the other skills of the Sales Boss they create a powerful motivating force. Be creative with how you fill people's motivational needs and tie them to sales achievement.

In addition to creating an environment that encourages action and motivation, a Sales Boss also understands the power of negative motivation. Withholding approval or imposing sanctions or punishments has the power to create change, but with lingering damage to the individual and the team. Negative approaches also lose their effectiveness over time. Think about a family situation in which the parent is always ranting or raising her voice about one thing or another. What happens to the kids over time? Eventually, they come to ignore the extreme emotions of the parent. But what happens if the parent is always calm and collected, but on rare occasions raises her voice? Suddenly the parent has the entire attention of the child. Use the negative side of motivation as sparingly as possible, and when/if you use it, do so only because you intend to use it and not simply because you have lost your composure.

In summary, first, the Sales Boss posts results publicly and makes sure the metrics posted create focus on the behaviors that will drive the desired selling outcome. Second, the Sales Boss discovers what motivates people on an individual level and designs a plan to feed that need. Before you move on from this chapter, think about the people on your team. Can you write down what motivates each of them? Can you identify why you believe that is the person's motivation? What evidence could you present of that motivation? Finally, do you have a plan in place to create the proper environment for motivated performers?

# 15

# Lead by Principle, Not Policy

remember walking into a prospective client's office and being impressed by how exquisite the decor was. It was like what you would imagine a very high-end attorney's offices would look like, with expensive hardwoods and finishes. Before meeting with the client, I asked whether I could use the restrooms. The restrooms were equally nice! What was odd though was a paper sign taped to the mirror: "Please wash your hands." Another sign was crudely taped to the door: "Did you remember to flush?" As I was led back to the offices, there were similar signs with reminders beside the copier, in the break room, and in other areas outlining behavior.

My question is: How many people were not flushing the toilet to make the need for a sign? How many were not washing their hands, putting their dishes away, or filling the paper tray on the copier?

My guess is that only a few people created this problem, but rather than address those offenders the person in charge made up signs and rules for everyone. I see the same habit in some sales managers. There might be an issue with one person, but rather than address that issue they'll issue a new rule or policy to the entire team. This is not the way of the Sales Boss.

The best Sales Bosses lead by principle rather than rules. They trust their team to make good decisions. When someone acts out of harmony with the company's principles, then they handle it on a case-by-case basis. For example, in many sales organizations, there is a stipulated per-diem that is paid to the salespeople when they travel overnight. The company might stipulate how much can be spent on hotel, breakfast, lunch, and dinner, or even treating a prospective client. Many times there is tension between the salesperson and the manager, as disagreements arise over whether the amount is adequate for the area they are traveling in.

One company handled this differently. They simply set the principle that, when it came to travel, the company is frugal so that more of the money earned can be paid out in actual benefits. The budget for travel that was allocated but not used would be rolled over into other company programs. This was the principle. They didn't set any rules. What they also did was publish publicly each month the average amount each salesperson spent on a night's hotel and meals. What do you think happened to the big spenders' habits? Over time, they took control of their spending and an average soon emerged as the norm for overnight expenses. Interestingly, this "norm" was less than the amount the company would have stipulated if they had made rules, and nobody was ever upset that the amount allocated wasn't fair or adequate.

How far you take the position of setting principles rather than rules may depend on the culture of your company, but use your influence to go as far toward leading by principle as possible. Remember that outside of the office your salespeople lead and manage every aspect of their lives, and most are fully capable of managing themselves responsibly at work when they understand the principles. Some companies have taken this so far as to not have a set number of vacation days or set work hours, and they rely on the principle that people will work hard to get the task done and live a balanced life. What they have discovered is that people very rarely abuse the system.

Think about the change in work habits since smart phones have become a part of our lives. Our employees end up being "on" all of the time. They take care of their prospects and clients nearly any hour of the day or night. Stipulating exact hours for work should be reserved for inside sales positions that require it. Outside traveling salespeople will, by the nature of the job, have long travel days and be away from home. Your company gets almost 24 hours of their time every day. On the weeks they've traveled heavily, does it make sense that you would ask them to come in on Friday and stay until 5 p.m.? You should give them the flexibility to reclaim some personal time for themselves and their families. Require them in the office only if you have an important meeting and a real reason they are needed that day. This isn't a day off; they've put in their time and are reclaiming that time.

While we are talking about principles rather than rules related to travel, I believe it is important to give some additional thought to what we require from our sales teams. The highest performing teams do not require travel away from home for a salesperson every week. I have watched many companies implement an out on Monday return late Thursday or early Friday, then repeat the next week, schedule. If this is the rhythm of your team, it will have bad long-term consequences. Some of these include:

- Poor planning and preparation for selling activities
- Poor follow-up on leads
- Exhaustion and weaker sales performance

Nobody wants to sustain that lifestyle once he gets married and has kids, so your best people will eventually decide to go to work for a company with a more balanced schedule. The only salespeople who will stay on your team long term are the ones who fear they don't have any better options—your poorest performers, your cats.

To summarize: Use principles instead of rules when possible. We've discussed Sacred Rhythms; these are the things that are unbreakable and inflexible. Everything else should have some leeway. When you use principles correctly, the team appreciates the balance and doesn't mind that you take seriously the Sacred Rhythms you've put in place.

# Make Sales Technology Work for You

've never met a salesperson who loved doing the administrative tasks of entering data or providing reports to management. However, you and the rest of the management team need to see the activity of the individuals on the sales team so you can forecast, predict inventory, and for an entire host of other reasons. When it comes to the sales team fully adopting sales technology, you will struggle unless you get it right from the beginning.

Think about the technology from the start as a way to increase the team's effectiveness and simplify the many tasks that they have to accomplish. Your mindset and belief must be that this is for *them* and not for you or the rest of the management team. Yes, the management team needs the data, but don't just build the system to be easy for you. Make it easy for the sales team.

First, make sure the team knows that it is important to use the system, and that it is *not* optional. Automate reminders to them when critical data are missing. For instance, if they haven't logged into the system for some days or if their forecasts run behind, the system can be set to ping them with reminders. When the automated system pings them, it is viewed as a reminder. When a person reminds them, it can be seen as nagging.

You will also need to have some increasing penalties in place for not using the system. I have seen companies include penalties such as reducing eligible commissions by a point or excluding a repeat offender from the company bonus pool. Chasing the team to get them to utilize the system isn't an option. If they want to be on the team, they use it. In extreme cases, I would go so far as to dismiss a salesperson if he or she consistently refused to use the system after appropriate coaching. I might offer the option of hiring an administrative assistant to do the work if someone is a real star and not replaceable.

The critical thing is to get the data you need to help inform your running of the team. Do not, however, run your team from behind the CRM! If you spend more than an hour a day combing through the CRM, you might want to reconsider how you use it. Those pretty graphs never sold anything.

Next, make sure that your system is user-friendly, does not require duplicate entry of data, and makes their jobs easier. Don't ask them for information they've already put into the system that you could simply look up. I've seen sales managers ask their people to keep the pipeline up-to-date and the salespeople do so, only to have the manager call them and ask, "What do you think will close this month?" The manager could have simply looked at the dashboard! If a sales manager wants to discuss the pipeline, then it should be on a deeper level during the monthly pipeline review. Have you ever sat through a PowerPoint presentation where someone just read you the slides? Was it frustrating? Likewise, it is frustrating for the salespeople if you have a meeting where they just read back to you what is on the screen of the CRM after they took the time to enter the data.

There is a wide range of tools for sales teams, and a full review is beyond the scope of this book. However, I will give you some checklists to consider when evaluating your systems and making enhancements.

Perhaps the largest tool the team will interact with is your CRM. This is where all the names of your customers live, along with all the information you have and will accumulate about them. The options range from the simple to the intricately complex. Your CRM should allow at a minimum:

- Tracking of sales opportunity
- Monthly pipeline and forecasts

- Automated follow-up tasks
- Automated logging of phone calls and all emails (from all mobile devices)
- Appointment coordination and scheduling
- Entering prospects into targeted marketing funnels (emails and direct mail)
- Access to the latest marketing collateral: videos, print, electronic
- Bid, quote, or proposal generation
- Sales dashboards
- Leads database and research portal
- Voice data entry
- Customer portal: issue resolution, etc.
- Mapping capability if fieldwork is required
- An auto-dialer if a majority of selling is on the phone
- Lead scoring
- Contact aging (lets you know whether an important contact hasn't been visited in a while)

If you need to see what a modern CRM system should look like and the capabilities, you can visit salesforce.com to see one of the leading solutions. YouTube has many videos of their system.

If you are a small business, you might consider Infusion-soft, which is leading the way in how small businesses follow up with their customers and prospects. Also, the leading players in the CRM space have an ecosystem of plugins created by outside vendors that will expand the usefulness of the system and help customize it for your particular need or industry.

The key is that the system should be powerful, yet simple. It should allow each salesperson to configure the workspace to match his or her style of working. When the system is simple, your team will use it willingly, as they'll see the difference it makes in their effectiveness. If your system is so out-of-date that it resembles something you'd encounter at your local driver's license office, then you'll need to advocate for a change. Until a change can be implemented, you will need to find the least painful workarounds for your sales team and openly admit to them that the system is archaic.

Another tool is email. Email has become so ubiquitous we rarely think about how we use it, and yet, according to one estimate, most people spend up to 75 percent of their work time reading, writing, and responding to email! This is an area where you can help the team reclaim some of their time.

Before jumping into managing the flood of emails, we should note that a Sales Boss doesn't sit behind his desk firing off email demands requesting updates or chiding some performance. Use email sparingly. Reserve email for an exchange of information and use the phone or face-to-face discussions whenever you can. The sound of your salesperson's voice will tell you things that no email could.

The most forward-looking teams have evolved away from email for much of their internal communication. Let me explain why. Have you ever been on a chain email where five or more people are copied? And everyone replies "all" and attaches versions of the latest document? By the time you get to the string of emails, you are lucky to sort it all out and make sure you haven't missed something critical! Sometimes we get so overloaded we simply quit reading them all. There is a much better way. You should consider using tools such as Chatter or Slack for all group communication. If you haven't used these yet, research the possibilities.

They work much like our social media feeds work, but for business. You can follow (the way you would on Twitter) people or projects. For instance, if you have a project going on with XYZ Company, you can start a feed called "XYZ Company Project."

Anyone with permission can view this "feed," comment, upload the latest files, and other processes. Marketing, engineering, sales, and service can all stay on the same page. Everything is in one place and organized with the latest data. Nothing gets lost in the email pile. Need someone on your team to take notice and action? You simply mention them using @name and they get a notice right on their smart phones. Advanced systems even allow your customers to be involved in feeds. When a new team member is added, he or she can get up to speed quickly on existing projects.

Clean out your email clutter by using a group-messaging tool. Don't be intimidated by this new technology, as it is simple to use and will alleviate a big headache. Younger employees will take to this system intuitively, as they've been raised using such tools in their personal lives.

For the remainder of the stuff in your inbox, teach your salespeople some email etiquette. This is as simple as what to put in the subject line and when to CC everyone or not. One company I worked with has these simple rules:

The subject line of each internal email starts with an indication describing the response needed:

- NRN means "No response needed, but needs to be looked at."
- URGENT means "Urgent Response Today." (If a response is needed in hours, the phone is used.)
- Respond (week/month/any).
- FYI means "Information shared out of possible interest."

This abbreviation is followed by a description of what is contained in the email. An example might be "NRN: Summary of last week's visit with Thompson & Co."

On all emails, a response is only required from people on the "To" line, not the "CC" line. Responses should only be to the person originating the email and not a "Reply all." If everyone on the email would benefit from seeing all the responses, the originator, after receiving all the responses, sends out a summary email to the entire group with the group's comments, for example: "NRN: Summary of the group's ideas for the company picnic."

Even better, these group emails would be moved into Slack. com's application. For longer topics, the phone should be used instead. If a subject is time critical, a phone call or text message is preferred. You will be amazed at the time and energy you will save if you take the time to teach your team how to use email and other communication tools appropriately.

Consider using a file-naming convention for any documents shared internally at the company, whether via email or on company intranets. Much time is wasted trying to locate and identify the right document at the time you need it. If you have a handful of salespeople sending you documents, it can quickly become a disaster! I once was looking for a PowerPoint presentation and found these in my file folder on the computer:

- Sales Presentation
- Sales Presentation Chicago
- Sales Presentation Version Two
- Sales Presentation Final Version
- Sales Presentation Final Final Version
- Sales Presentation Last Version

Can you guess how many files I had to look through to find the right presentation? All of them. And then I found the right file: Chicago Final Sales Presentation!

A file-naming convention just means we agree as a group on how to name a file. One company uses this pattern:

{Descriptive Name}.{Version #}.{date}.{Initials of Author}

Chicago Final Sales Presentation becomes:

ChicagoSalesPresentation.V5.Sept2015.JW

The Weekly Sales Report becomes:

SalesReport.Sept2015.JW

Customer Quotes becomes:

Quote.XYZCompany.V2.Sept2015.JW

When implemented, this system makes it easy for me to find the latest sales report from anybody on my team or the quote for my customer. Create good digital housekeeping rules and your job will become much easier. It helps teach people to be organized in the way they run their business. It takes a bit of effort on the front end getting people disciplined enough to develop new habits, but it will save much time, energy, and effort in the future. While it may seem insignificant to spend time considering how we handle the exchange and storing of information within our sales team and company, it is an area the Sales Boss will recognize as having an impact on results. The ease and speed of exchanging important information will allow you to serve your customers more effectively, create less frustration and fewer mistakes, and free up time that can be used for selling face-to-face with prospects. Without fail, when I have seen a high-performing team there has always been obvious structure in the way they communicate.

# Money Talks

## Compensation Planning

M ost people who make a career out sales do so because, among other things, they know that sales is where the money is. Your ability to design a plan that moves all of the right levers is intrinsic to your success. As we jump into a talk about compensation, I'll make two initial observations:

1. In some companies a jealousy develops between the other members of the company and the salespeople. The finance people and some of the other executives see the "outsized" paychecks of the top performers and don't see them reporting into the office. As they see the salesperson's compensation surpass their own, they get jealous. This behavior will show up in many ways. You might start noticing executives in the finance or HR department nitpicking each and every expense report. You'll hear sarcasm from them when mentioning that a salesperson landed a nice size deal. They'll say things like "Well, that customer was going to buy anyway. They didn't do anything special." When you notice these behaviors, you will need to be proactive. Your job is to make sure the entire company knows how tough it is out in the field doing sales, the sacrifice in time away from family, and other challenges the salesperson endures. They earn their money, and the entire company eats because the salesperson closed a deal. Make sure nobody forgets or begrudges the hand that feeds them.

2. Make sure you aren't overpaying. This may seem like a contrasting statement; however, your company should only be paying as much as it takes to keep the best in the industry. Some jobs are only worth so much. When you

overpay you are taking away from funds that could be used for research and development, new equipment, marketing, or technology innovations. The proper plan balances the need to keep great people with the need to retain and reinvest revenue in other parts of the company. You can strike the right balance by looking at compensation studies to see what your competition is paying. Companies such as ERI provide this service (erieri.com). Don't rely on free services on the Internet or "the word" of a recruiter. Pay the few hundred dollars it will take to get a scientific and data-rich report. Also, when you hire salespeople from other companies, if you are following our guidelines, you are asking to see their historical earnings verified by their W-2s or other payroll records, so you will start seeing patterns in the industry that will back up your report. We'll talk more on setting a range in a bit.

An entire book could be written about compensation planning, and indeed many great ones have, which you might also look to for help. In this chapter, I will simply highlight what should be considered best practices and what I've seen work or fail to work in the plans I've witnessed. After reading this, you'll have the foundation for a plan that works to drive selling success.

Compensation plans should always be as simple as possible for your team to understand on the individual salesperson level. However, if the holistic plan is complex due to the nature of your company, with several layers of sales teams, then you would be well served to consider bringing in a compensation expert who can help you consider all of the ramifications of the various options and the legal consequences of each. In most companies, crafting an effective plan is well within the capabilities of the executive team as long as you follow some of the basic principles shared in this chapter.

Here are the top four things that must be true about any plan:

1. Your compensation plan allows you to attract, retain, and even steal superstar salespeople from your competition. It keeps your stars happy.
2. It connects to the longer-term strategy of your organization while not penalizing the team.
3. It is simple to understand, and each measure is directly tied to something within the salesperson's control.
4. There must be a wide margin between the total comp of star performers and that of average performers.

Finding real superstars is difficult, and you should never risk losing a star because of some inequality or flaw of your compensation plan. Your compensation plan will influence how your team spends its time. Carefully consider the intended and unintended consequences your plan will have on team behavior. For instance, a plan that strongly incentivizes opening new accounts could serve the unintended consequence of team members ignoring existing customers and failing to grow the depth of products sold into these customers. If this happens, what is your plan for dealing with this unintended outcome?

Comcast serves as a cautionary story for what can happen when a compensation plan is built on the wrong premise. Comcast designed a plan that incentivized sales reps if they were able to convince a customer who was calling to cancel a cable subscription to stick with the company instead of canceling. The Internet was soon flooded with recorded phone calls that frustrated consumers had when they were strong-armed by Comcast reps who did everything they could to keep people from canceling so they could pocket a commission. If you Google "Comcast customer service calls frustrated," you can listen in on the unintended consequence that came from the decision to compensate this way.

When designing your plan, always consider how it will act once you release it into the wild! What will your team do with it in the pursuit of maximizing their income? Typically, a sales compensation plan consists of three parts: base salary, variable commissions, and bonuses. Let's define the key aspects of each area.

## Base Salary

This is the portion of your salesperson's compensation that is guaranteed. I have encountered many companies that wish to have a "commission only" sales position, thinking that it limits the risk the company takes in hiring a new salesperson. While this might seem true, it rarely works out that way. Usually, this method is chosen because a company lacks the ability or discipline to make great hiring decisions and offers little training. You will never build or attract a superstar this way. A star salesperson knows his or her worth and will always have the option for a job that has some base built into the plan. If you are building a sales team, always include a base salary when the team member is starting with the company. You might choose to have this base salary decrease with time as the salesperson builds up a book of business and has a consistent level of commissions, but your plan should be designed in a way that doesn't make this seem like it is punishing success. Some companies have simply given a higher base rate during the training time period and a lower commission, then give the sales reps the initiative to choose when they move to a higher commission level and sacrifice the base pay.

# Variable Commissions

This is the portion of compensation that is based on selling or some other revenue-generating activity performed by the salesperson. This should be tied to things the salesperson directly impacts. For instance, if you have "appointment setters" who pass the appointment on to a field salesperson, they'd receive a commission on setting the appointment, regardless of how the deal ended, since they don't directly impact the close, whereas the field person would only receive a commission on closing the deal, not setting the appointment.

A word of caution is in order here: When you choose these variables, you must be certain that your company can accurately and in a timely way measure and report on them. You don't want to be arguing with your team or making judgment calls when it comes to how things are calculated.

# Bonuses

Bonuses can be actual compensation or other incentives that are included to influence certain types of activity. An example of this would be when a company pays a one-time amount for each customer the salesperson closes who has not previously purchased from the company. This can also take the form of non-cash incentives. You often hear of reward trips and other spiffs. One company I know leases a high-end luxury car and the keys are passed each quarter to the person who has the largest percentage gain in new customers. I can tell you the team really competes to see who'll be driving in style! If you can have some over-the-top perk for someone who is number one in whatever behavior you are trying to incentivize (not always the top earner), you will see a big impact on the team. Give it some thought and creativity.

How do we set the total compensation and what is the right mix? In HR circles, you will hear the term TTC, meaning "total target compensation." Here is what it means for setting your team's compensation: Your entire mix of compensation (base, variable, bonus) should equal a target amount. This target should be set based on the industry compensation study I mentioned previously using the 90th percentile (meaning this level is above 90 percent of others in the industry). Then adjust it this way: Calculate your plan based on your company's historical sales-people's sales so that 50 percent of the team would have achieved the TTC, 30 percent would fail to reach the TTC level, and 20 percent would exceed the level.

What this means in practice is that your superstars will not only far out-earn the bottom people on their team, but they will also be significantly better compensated than any of their industry peers and you'll be at no risk of losing them. Your middle performers (who, if you are doing it right, are still pretty darn good) will be making as much as they could in most places, so likely won't leave. Your bottom performers will do OK (remember that we don't keep cats), but they will have incentive to keep stretching themselves. Everybody is happy.

The gap between your very best performers and your bottom performers should be significant, as this will drive the hunger to keep performing and improving skills. Remember that I suggested posting results publicly. If you have hired correctly, you won't have people who are content knowing they left some money on the table. This doesn't mean that you have "low performers" or cats, it just means that the very best have the ability to really distinguish themselves, and you might even see the names at the top of the list change places with those on the bottom from quarter to quarter and year to year. In fact, if you have someone who is always in the bottom and failing to reach the TTC level, then you likely have someone you should consider replacing.

Now that we have set the TTC, the second thing is how to decide what the mix should be among base, variable, and bonus. The basic answer is that the higher the skill needed to close the business and the more impact the salesperson's activity has on the outcome, the more the compensation should be weighted in the variable component. The lower the impact, the higher the base should be. In the latter case, the TTC would also usually be lower. Using this formula allows you to pay the highest compensation levels when the highest level of skill is needed and to control costs when the job is more on the level of "order taking" than selling.

A more skillful art is making sure that no salesperson can live comfortably in the lifestyle he or she is accustomed to on the base salary you provide. Here is where your knowing how much is "a lot of money" in the eyes of your new salesperson is critical. You will want to make sure that the salesperson's lifestyle can only be maintained by exceeding sales targets. This is both science and art. The reason should be obvious and goes back to understanding what makes humans work. All of us tend to slow down our efforts when we reach a level of comfort. I know that in my own case I used to have no problem putting in fifteen-hour days and traveling non-stop for business. I was hungry and trying to establish myself. Now, as I have reached a level of comfort and success and no longer worry about where the next mortgage payment is coming from, it is a bit more difficult to want to hit the road so hard. You and your salespeople are the same. The only difference between humans is what level they need to be at to hit the "comfortable" button and slow their activity. Make sure the base that you provide doesn't allow them to reach that button. You need everyone to stretch.

Some final best practices on compensation:

1. Don't change plans mid-year or suddenly. When you change plans mid-year, it interrupts the rhythm of your

team. Nothing is more personal than how a person gets paid, and even if the change is good, it will distract some of the mental energy your team should be spending on selling. Teams typically expect changes at the end of a year, so leverage this expectation when you need to make changes by choosing this time of year and by talking early about the upcoming changes and why they are being made. Also, you'll want to avoid changes that will negatively affect the amount a person earns when performing at the same level as in the past. If you must make these types of negative impact changes, plan to use your EQ and be as authentic as possible when sharing the business reasons why a change must take place.

2. Always issue the plan before the time period it covers. (I've seen companies issue a plan six months into the year, all the while the sales team is wondering how they get paid!)

3. Pay any variable comp as close to the pay period where the sale closed as possible. I call this the Pavlov dog principle. You want them connecting the bump in their bank deposit to the sales event and the behaviors that created the sale. Sometimes, companies wait till the invoice is paid, which can be six months after the sale happened. This isn't ideal. If your company chooses to reduce risk by waiting until funds are received on a sale and the collection process is lengthy, you might try offering a partial bonus immediately on reporting and the remainder when the funds are fully received. The key is to have the salesperson "feel it in the bank account" while actively doing all of the right behaviors so a stronger connection is made.

4. Have a dashboard or some other method of communicating exactly what they are being paid for, how much they are owed, and how it has been calculated. I've had sales guys not understand how they were being paid or just be

randomly surprised when the bonus funds showed up in their accounts. You want them to be absolutely certain of what it takes to move the money needle for their families. When you create certainty on how they are being paid, it has the side effect of demonstrating how behaviors such as discounting to close the sale impact their paychecks.

5. Don't have more than a couple of items being measured for variable commissions or bonuses, and make sure they are things that are readily visible and easily measured.

I'm often asked about a couple of other areas related to compensation, so here are my thoughts and the reasoning behind them.

## What about "house accounts"?

When clients ask me about house accounts, they typically mean some book of business or customers who existed prior to the salesperson's involvement. The concern is usually that the salesperson didn't have to initially bring this business in the door, and my client feels that he or she shouldn't be paid on the business and so has labeled a handful of clients as house accounts. While this is understandable, I think it is shortsighted to completely block these accounts from a new salesperson. The key reason is that house accounts typically represent some of the oldest and most loyal customers, and because of this, serve as a rich source of referrals and leads. If we block the salespeople from profiting from these accounts, we also reduce the ability and incentive for them to establish meaningful relationships with these customers. As a result, the level of referrals is never optimized. I would suggest that salespeople take full responsibility for house accounts, but for a period of time the level of commission based on direct sales into these companies be reduced, with a path to full commissions after they've completely assumed and solidified relationships with the existing customers and when the customer has indicated trust in the salesperson by offering referrals and new business opportunities that didn't exist previously. This balance usually has the best outcome for everyone.

## How should we pay on consumables or parts?

Consumables refer to products that are used up and reordered on a regular basis. For instance, a company might sell a piece of equipment that requires utilizing some type of packaging, chemical, or parts that wear out on a regular basis and must be replaced. Some companies include these consumables or parts in the compensation plan and others exclude them. I think that if the salespeople have or could have a measure of influence on the amount consumed, then they should be paid on the consumable. These consumables can form a bit of annuity for the established salesperson and serve as a wonderful recruiting tool when competing for the best salespeople.

The danger is that, after a period of working hard, a salesperson might reach a level of comfort that comes from the income on these consumable annuities each year and slow down on hunting for new business. As the Sales Boss, you will need to monitor this tendency and have an appropriate plan in place to counter it. I have seen companies accomplish a balance by having the annuity payment percentage reduce in subsequent years. For instance, if they pay out 5 percent of consumable orders in year one to the salesperson, then over a period of five years that percentage may reduce to 1 percent as the customer's buying behavior becomes entrenched and less effort is needed from the salesperson.

• • •

As we end this discussion on compensation, it should also be noted that it isn't always necessary or preferable to have money be the only form of incentive. Think of it this way: if you were to give a bonus of a few thousand dollars to an employee, for how long would the employee remember it? I would say for a very short period of time. What would happen if, instead of the cash, you offered a menu of vacations from which to pick? How long would the employee remember that? Likely, forever. Certainly during the few days people are on the beach with their families, they'd be filled with positive feelings about their jobs and your company. They'd remember it each time they looked at the pictures and they'd relive it each time they recounted stories of the trip to their friends. When they returned to the office, they'd posses a level of energy that would pay dividends to the rest of the team. When a headhunter comes to take your best salespeople, those people will remember the emotions and not the pay. As a Sales Boss, give some serious thought to how you might utilize non-cash compensation. It will increase the feeling of employee belonging and is a powerful tool to build your team's cohesiveness.

CHAPTER

# 18

# Forecasting the Future

One of the necessary evils of being the Sales Boss is forecasting revenue. To say that forecasting is the bane of existence for most sales managers is an understatement. I would go so far as to say that if a sales manager had a choice to complete the forecast or go to the dentist for a root canal, then the sales manager might just have a monthly visit to the dentist! The term "forecast" is used differently in different sales organizations, but broadly speaking, it is the crystal ball that a company asks the sales manager to look into to predict what revenue will be produced, from which channels the revenue will come, and when the company can expect it to show up on the books. Sometimes this is the sales budget prepared at the beginning of the year, followed by changes and updates through the rest of the year.

Most sales managers struggle to get the forecast right. The one thing that can be said with certainty is that the forecast is only accurate as a reflection of the hopes the sales manager has on the day it is submitted. I tend to think of it as a list of gifts a child writes for Santa Claus. Some of those gifts are received, some are a surprise under the tree, and some, like world peace, clearly didn't ever stand a chance of happening, but were on the list anyway just in case this year was different!

Why are forecasts notoriously difficult? To begin with, forecasting is a battle between two opposing forces: reality and the desire to look good. When you ask your salespeople what they feel will close, the tendency is to be optimistic. When you are asked to provide next year's numbers you know the C-level won't be happy with a line that trends down or goes only slightly uphill. It's easy to submit the optimistic number and spend the next twelve months chasing it.

The second challenge with getting the number right is having accurate and meaningful data. The problem with forecasting wrong is that it throws off the rest of the planning the company might undertake. It also hurts your credibility as the team falls short each month. It is imperative that you try to get as close as possible. I tend to think of "close" as being within 10 and 20 percent on a month-by-month basis. Of course, this percentage really depends on the scale of the number you are forecasting. If you want to produce better forecasts, it is incumbent upon you as the Sales Boss to take a different approach than just a routine inspection of the numbers modified by a gut feel.

If you have followed the advice in this book so far, you'll already be well positioned to improve your forecasts. This is because you have a unified sales process across the team, you have good data in your CRM, and you have had regular coaching sessions with the team and accompanied them in the field. Having a deep connection to the team will have sharpened your sense of how real the numbers are.

I remember starting a project with a new client who had historically had a terrible time coming up with an accurate forecast. I was brought on board very close to the time sales budgets were submitted and was asked to provide a sales number for the new year. I'm not certain why they thought my number would be better than the existing team's missed guesses from past years. I gathered some data and made the forecast. Everyone was surprised when I was within $2,000 each month for three months on numbers that exceeded $1.5 million. How did I do it? Here was the secret: If nothing changes, then nothing changes. What this means is that, unless you have changed something within your company or something within the economy has changed, then you'll likely have the same results as previously. This isn't what people want to hear, but it is the truth!

Sometimes companies forecast a 25 to 35 percent growth rate but don't plan to do anything different. I'm not sure why they are surprised when they don't see the growth. What I had done in this case was look at the last three years' actual sales totals. I looked at the sales individually and subtracted anything that was an anomaly or something that was a "one-time surprise." This gave me a base number. I figured out what the average "one-time surprises" were and added that number back in. The result was an accurate forecast. If nothing changes, then nothing changes.

You should use a similar strategy when forecasting your numbers. Get a solid baseline, ask yourself "What has changed?," and then account for this change. When you identify something that has or will change in the upcoming year, avoid being optimistic about the impact this will have on revenue. Pick a number based on your best data, and then look at past changes. What was the difference between expected and actual revenue? How far off were the predictions? What was the average percentage the team was off by? Adjust your number by that percentage.

Good forecasting requires you to understand your buyers' behavior. It is incumbent on you to understand what is happening in your customers' world and how they are making their buying decisions. As you have implemented the earlier suggestions, you will have discovered a series of milestones that your customers typically go through—a certain percentage that are at one milestone will move to the next and a certain percentage will fall out. Use this number to inform your forecast. Recognize that the process of forecasting should always be changing and, as you learn, you'll get better at producing a reliable number that can help you lead and manage the business and decide how to allocate resources.

When you come up with a number through a data-driven and thoughtful process, don't adjust the number just because someone else on the executive team doesn't like it. If he or she wants the number to be higher, go back to my adage: If nothing changes, nothing changes. You might tell the other executives that you'd be happy to raise the number, but something will have to change. Are they prepared to invest in additional marketing, tradeshows, salespeople, etc.? Arbitrary numbers will have unintended consequences. If there is a difference of opinion on what the number should be, be willing to fight up front about it. It is better to fight up front than to chase an unrealistic number the rest of the year. Forecasting correctly at the start, you will have created great value for your company, enhanced your trustworthiness, and made your job much easier in the process.

CHAPTER

# 19

# Replicating Success

A s the Sales Boss, you have the broadest view of all of the things that impact sales success. Indeed, if you are doing your job well, you have a better feel for the pulse of the company than anyone else, including the CEO. You have access to the company's budgets; you review the marketing plans, and perhaps even sit in on some of the operations meetings. You are in the field with your salespeople and see the widest segment of companies across different geographies and market segments. Be aware of the unique insights this gives you and the ability to see how everything fits together. Remember that things that might seem obvious to you (because of the plethora of information available to you) might seem less obvious to others in your company. Be ready to make the case for things that will help replicate successes across the organization. It is not unusual for other departments to make decisions based on the silo that they exist in every day, and you bring real value to the organization when you are able to relate stories from the field.

For instance, you might discover through your regular calls with the sales team that there is a new competitor in the field that is gaining traction due to a unique product feature or positioning. Would recounting these stories to the marketing and product development teams prove valuable? Would additional research be warranted? You might understand from your discussions with your finance department that the margins on one of your key products have shrunk dramatically or that the cost to support the product makes the segment less attractive. Would refocusing the prospecting efforts of your sales team to other products impact the overall profitability of the company? When marketing launches a new campaign, do you communicate that to the sales team so they can leverage the exposure? Do you provide feedback to marketing if their efforts produce the wrong type of leads? I hope you can see the need to reach into other areas of the company for the benefit of your team.

An area you can focus on that will help you to replicate success is *territory planning*. Your salespeople will tend to focus on areas that they are most comfortable selling to. Typically, this will come from the areas they have had the most success in or that they feel the most knowledgeable about. For instance, one of my clients sells equipment that can be utilized both in the medical field and also in food processing. When they hire a salesperson, the salesperson can sometimes focus almost entirely on one of the segments and ignore the others due to his or her own past experience. Perhaps the salesperson has a medical background and so calls on medical companies, while a co-worker ends up selling entirely to food companies because she is comfortable calling on plant engineers. Your role is to make sure that you have clearly defined the profile of appropriate targets in each territory and then have aligned the efforts of the team to target those accounts. You should analyze the past successes of the team and build a profile of the most profitable and probable types of prospects so that you can replicate those wins.

A company should be able to say with clarity: "Our best customers are $x$–size, are involved in this type of business, have these kinds of problems, and are most likely to buy when this event has happened or is about to happen." This clarity will allow your team to replicate success consistently. When you are coaching a salesperson, you may discover a trend that has led to greater success by a member of your team. When this happens, make sure to develop a case study that can be shared that details why this trend is impacting sales and how the team members can leverage the trend to win new business. What questions should they be asking? What news sources or organizations should they be tuned into to identify prospects? Formalize the process of sharing insights about what is working, rather than leave it to the grapevine.

When thinking about how to replicate success, think about aligning with people outside the walls of your company. Ask yourself: "Who are the companies that sell to the same customers or at the same events as we do, but sell a different product?" For instance, if you are a company that sells equipment into new construction projects, you might identify folks who sell insurance, security, temp workers, or other products and services. This can happen regardless of industry. There is always some company that shares your target prospect. How do you leverage that company's marketing and relationships to your advantage? It should be your goal to create formal referral networks with these parallel industries. Require your salespeople to arrange and chair these lead groups.

Here is how it works: Draw up a list of types of companies that are parallel to yours and who call at the same level in the organization as your team. For example, if you need to call on the CEO, you wouldn't consider a parallel company to be someone who calls on operations or vice versa. A parallel company is one that has the same type of prospect companies *and* calls at the same level in the company. Once you develop a list of five to ten companies, research who the best salesperson is for those companies in the region that your salesperson is covering. For instance, if I have my team split into five regions, I will have a list of five salespeople's names from the parallel company. For the sake of discussion, let's pretend you have a Midwest sales region. You've identified seven parallel companies and now have seven names of those companies' salespeople. Reach out and invite these salespeople to participate in a leads group. Arrange for your salesperson to host a lunch or breakfast in the region once a month in a place convenient to the group. You want this to be face-to-face. During this meeting all participants will make it their goal to share intelligence on the companies and prospects that they are calling on. Invariably, each of the salespeople will have different relationships and have called on different targets than the others.

As the group develops friendships and trust with each other, they'll become good sources of leads. This is like having seven extra sets of eyes out in your target market. Because you are calling on a similar market, your salesperson should make it a point at these meetings to position him- or herself as a trusted advisor knowledgeable about the industry and come prepared to share a recent industry trend or something else that will prove valuable to the rest of the group. As the Sales Boss, you might even provide these talking points or ask for help from your marketing team.

The key idea is that, as your salespeople give of themselves at these hosted events, they'll quickly establish themselves as people to be trusted, and the other salespeople will want to reciprocate by providing value in return. It's human nature. There is nothing better than when one of the members of the lead group calls and says, "Hey, I was in at XYZ company and I noticed that they are expanding into X. This would be the perfect time for you to reach out to them. Do you have a relationship with Jim already or shall I introduce the two of you?" That's replicating success. Don't leave it to your sales team to decide whether this is something they'll do. Make it mandatory and part of the expectations for managing the territory. It pays huge dividends.

A final area to consider is how you position your team as experts. In this age of Google, most customers will have done some research and formed an impression about your company and your salesperson prior to buying or engaging with you. To the extent possible, find ways to have your salespeople be viewed as experts in the community. This means speaking on panels at conferences, writing articles in trade journals, or posting relevant material on LinkedIn. The goal is that when prospects have a problem, they think of your team as the experts. I have found that this is a weak area in most companies. It is a gray area that lives between sales and marketing, so no one takes full responsibility for its execution. You, the Sales Boss, own and nurture the process. A side benefit is that, as the community starts to see one of your salespeople as an expert, the confidence of the salesperson is also increased and the sale becomes easier because the client is less susceptible to applying pricing pressure.

Live with your radar on high alert and find the opportunities to replicate success. There are always clues about what made things happen. Your job as Sales Boss is to find them and replicate them.

CHAPTER

# 20

# The Business of You

S ales Bosses understand that, ultimately, they are self-employed and work for themselves. You must have the mindset of an entrepreneur who recognizes that success and failure are fully your responsibility. As the Sales Boss, you are in the business of you. No matter what company you have chosen to attach yourself to, your income is predicated on what you have done and what you have failed to do. You don't get credit for your sales plan or what you *intended* to do. You get credit for what you actually produce. Unlike almost any other role in the company, your value is measured by a black-and-white measuring stick of revenue generated for the company and, typically, you are only as good as your last quarter. Past wins are soon forgotten as the pressure of today's shortcoming in sales grows larger. The only remedy is sales. Sales fix everything. This is the reality of a Sales Boss's life. It takes a unique personality to be able to operate with this level of unending pressure, but the Sales Boss thrives in this environment.

Recognizing that you are in the business of you means that you take care of yourself mentally, physically, and emotionally. You are responsible for filling yourself up with the things that will inspire, refresh, and energize you. These things will give you the ability to give of yourself to the team. I'd like you to reflect for a minute on a couple of questions and, rather than simply read these questions, actually answer them.

## When was the last time you attended a non-work-related conference or training?

It is important that you expose yourself to trends in industries outside of the one you work in. None of our businesses exist in

235

a vacuum, and often the trends started in one industry eventu-ally bleed into others. By attending other conferences you give your mind the opportunity to make mental connections between sometimes seemingly unrelated things and you increase your mental flexibility.

## What was the last book or magazine you read?

A leader will always have a steady diet of thought fed through reading. Try to read from a wide range of sources. One of the chal-lenges with reading online is that the Internet has been designed to serve us information that the data says we are most likely to respond to. For instance, if you read political articles from con-servative sources, you'll start noticing that your Google searches will list conservative sources first when you are doing an Internet search. We can start to consume information in an echo cham-ber that feeds back and reinforces our own viewpoints. This leads to mental rigidity. I recommend consuming books, magazines, and web articles from as wide a range as possible. I subscribe to science magazines, travel magazines, psychology magazines, industry trade journals, lifestyle magazines, conservative news magazines, liberal news magazines, entrepreneurial magazines, and established business magazines such as *Forbes*. I read at least two books a month related to sales and a third book on a random topic. I have found that this buffet of information creates connec-tions in unexpected ways that have value to the work I am trying to accomplish. Try adding a little variety into your reading diet.

## What sacred time do you have set aside for you?

When I use the term "sacred time," it is similar to what I meant by Sacred Rhythms. What is the time that you have set aside just for you? The time you use to meditate, exercise, or reflect and plan? I suggest that you block this time on your calendar to signify its importance to you and to be intentional with how you use it. If you do have time set aside, are you using it effectively?

The time I have available to me most often is the early morning hours. I found that I was using this time for catching up on the news. It wasn't until someone asked me why I'd ever want to start my day that way that I started thinking about how much this routine had become a part of who I was. I decided to quit the routine of checking the news in the morning, but I still kept logging in. Frustrated, I decided to start taking notes on the news that I digested in the morning. The results were sobering; I'd on average consume twenty deaths, murders, and atrocities in the first thirty minutes. By the time I'd finished forty-five minutes, I'd learned about cheating, lying, embezzling, hunger, and genocide. That was enough to sober me up and make me quit cold turkey. I've been clean for a year. I replaced the morning ritual (addiction), with another ritual: writing and learning. It has proven to be a powerful 1–2 punch! The results surprised even me. Now with my first cup of coffee, I log into TED Talks and watch people dreaming, doing, and sharing amazing things. Once my mind wakes up and I am feeling inspired, I write.

This past year I wrote several guides related to my business expertise that have helped my clients and served as useful prospecting tools. I contributed to a book with Jack Canfield that hit number one best-seller on Amazon, and wrote this book that you hold in your hands today. I've kept up with my blogging. I've designed and launched several new products. After I write, I've started to log into Lynda.com and choose something to learn. So far I have learned the basics of PHP and how to use Adobe After Effects and InDesign. I've picked up some additional marketing know-how, learned some fundamental concepts regarding analyzing big data, podcasting, and creating a video studio. I've met some amazing people and attended some fantastic conferences as a result of the people I met from my new morning routines. I achieved all of this just by substituting my world news addiction for something healthier. I still check in on the news, but I do it while driving in the car through satellite radio. Make sure that the habits you have regarding the personal time you do have serve you well.

## What sacred time do you have set aside for your family?

The answer to this question is critically important. We don't get any do-overs. Our children, spouses, and families don't have a pause button. Most people who do well as a Sales Boss are successful because they love an environment that gives them immediate challenge, feedback, and success. They close a deal or help guide the team to the success of a deal. It feels good. We feel needed and relevant. We made it happen. Unfortunately, this same feedback loop of success that we become addicted to can make us neglect our personal relationships and family. It's easy to understand how answering the email, making the phone call, or getting on the plane leads to closing business and bringing in revenue. Our family life's success isn't as easily measured, and the feedback isn't as instantaneous. It's only after a period of neglect that the results show up in divorce, alienated kids, or poor relationships. The only way to guard against this danger is to have sacred time for your family. It's only after consistent attention that we have close personal and loving relationships.

Commit to yourself that you will not steal time and attention away from your family in the pursuit of being the Sales Boss. Don't make an exception "just this once," because you will soon learn that life is a series of exceptions. Your company doesn't own you because they pay you a salary. Shut your phone off in the evenings. Be fully present. Don't send out emails to your team late at night or respond to their emails. I know that this idea is unpopular in a world that seems to glorify 24/7 access.

The problem is that we value accessibility sometimes more than results. Be powerful, present, and results-driven at work, and then do the same for your family. Trust me when I say that your salespeople will have greater success if you insist they do the same. You don't own them either. If you give 100 percent of your time to your company or expect the same from your team, then you are in a vicious cycle of working-to-have-money-so-you-can-afford-a-place-to-sleep-so-you-can-go-back-to-work-to-afford-a-place-to-sleep. This is not a fun cycle. Decide that you will work so you can have a life.

## How do you relax?

This is important. How do you shut down and relax? Does your method leave you energized and refreshed? I find that many sales managers turn to alcohol to relax. If this is your prime method to relax, you will discover that it's not a sustainable solution. I'm not suggesting you not drink, but simply that I see many sales managers use alcohol to relieve the pressure they feel at work. Take an inventory of how you relax. Does it serve you well?

## Who is your mentor?

It has been said that we are the sum of the people we hang out with. If this is true, it highlights for us the importance of being mindful of whom we associate with. Do you have a mentor? Do you have someone who embodies a skill, a quality, or something else that you'd like to possess with whom you spend time as a mentee? Try to find someone who is operating at a level higher than you and spend time with that person. Have you ever played a sport with someone better than you? What happened? For a while, I liked to play racquetball. A curious thing happened when I played someone who was my equal. I would actually find my skills deteriorating and start to become bored! However, when I played someone better than I was, not only did my skills increase, but the enjoyment I got from the game was much higher—even though I lost a higher percentage of the games played. If you want to be great, play with people who are more skilled than you are.

As you thought through these questions, did you like your answers? Develop the habit of checking in from time to time on how well you are doing at caring for yourself. It is easy to get caught up in the routines of what we need to do each day as the Sales Boss and forget about our own needs. It is vital that you remember that your most important client is *you*. Without your mental and physical health, you cannot contribute what is most needed to the team. Just like physical diet and exercise, the better your mental diet and exercise, the happier and more successful you will be. Most sales managers reach a point at which they aren't upgrading their skills through books, conferences, mentoring groups, and other resources. The Sales Boss is aggressive about upgrading his or her knowledge and plugging into sources of energy. Because of this, the Sales Boss stands above the crowd. Because of this, the team can sense energy, enthusiasm, and intelligence, and it is easier for the Sales Boss to lead the team.

Let's get slightly more personal. If you were to stand in front of a mirror, what would you see? What would your physical appearance tell you? Your appearance is an accumulation of the choices that you have made. Let's be honest: age and time hit us all. While it may soften our edges and give us the look of wisdom, it can also be downright harsh. But look closer. Can you see the evidence of too many days spent behind a computer with little to no activity? Can you feel the strain in your joints? If you look, you'll find those late-night meals eaten on the run while you tried to fit in one more thing before the day came to an end and you again fell asleep exhausted, knowing you'd never get enough sleep before the cycle started again. You'll feel the time spent slaving over another important deadline: "I'm too busy to relax. I will sleep when I am dead." That's your mindset.

Here's the hard truth: You can't lead if you can't control your own life and health. I'm not suggesting every leader needs to be fit for the cover of a magazine or can't have health issues—we are all human, after all. I am suggesting that your leadership edge is duller when you forget to take time to be healthy and make the healthiest choices you can. Given a choice, nobody wants to follow a fat leader. I can say this because I've been fat and unhealthy. It doesn't have to "come with the territory." The Sales Boss recognizes that he or she is a billboard for the company. People will be influenced by what they see. Make sure that you are healthy, then choose clothing and personal grooming habits that say that you are the Sales Boss. Yes, you can manage people and sales without having this aspect buttoned up, but you'll never be a Sales Boss. You'll never operate at the highest level of results without getting this part of your world under control. Be healthy.

Honestly assessing your routines and habits as a leader is the critical starting point for improvement. We've discussed within the pages of this book the secrets to becoming a Sales Boss and what differentiates the extraordinary sales leader from the merely ordinary. So how did you do? The role of Sales Boss isn't easy, but it is filled with rewards. You aren't just helping companies sell more "stuff." A good Sales Boss leaves an indelible imprint on the lives of those he or she works with, inspiring them to be the best version of themselves. Sales Bosses help their teams grow and provide for their families in abundance. Nothing happens until someone sells something. No kids get sent to college, no homes get purchased, no diseases cured, and no vacations enjoyed. You are at the center of something special as the Sales Boss. Go build something great. Build a sales team. You have the secret. Being a Sales Boss is up to you.

# The Sales Boss Scorecard

If you are looking for a quick checklist to evaluate how great you are as a Sales Boss or you need to evaluate the manager of your sales team, then understand that you might be over-simplifying. Read through the pages of this book and spend thoughtful and honest time asking yourself how well you are doing in each of the areas below. You can use the checklist below as an ongoing evaluation to keep yourself on track, but it will be important to understand what the intent is behind each of the statements. For instance, the statement: "I provide a weekly coaching session" should be evaluated in light of how the coaching sessions are outlined in this book. Not all coaching is created equal.

## The Scorecard

### Chapter 1 The Work of a Sales Boss

- ☐ I accept full responsibility for my company's results, even when the results are negatively impacted by other departments' actions.
- ☐ I exceed revenue expectations.

## Chapter 2 The Importance of Sacred Rhythms

- ☐ I consider myself more a part of the management team than the sales team.
- ☐ My team understands the rhythms of the sales group.
- ☐ My rhythms are designed intentionally for achieving results.
- ☐ I have a reputation for attracting great salespeople.

## Chapter 3 The DNA of a Sales Boss

- ☐ I have the ability to identify and manage my emotions.
- ☐ I harness my emotions and apply them to problem solving and thinking.
- ☐ I have the ability to cheer people up or calm them down.
- ☐ I don't need the credit or seek it.
- ☐ I have a balanced and analytical mind.
- ☐ I inspire others.
- ☐ I can hold the attention of a room.
- ☐ I am comfortable sitting in judgment.
- ☐ I give uncomfortable feedback face-to-face rather than by email.
- ☐ I am actively engaged, not micro-managing.
- ☐ I am honest always. People aren't surprised by my positions.
- ☐ I am authentic.
- ☐ I am the thermostat, not the thermometer.
- ☐ I trust but verify what people tell me.
- ☐ I connect action to big ideas.

## Chapter 4 The Truth About Humans

- ☐ I am a student of human behavior.
- ☐ I am willing to get up close and personal to understand people.

☐ I know what motivates my people individually.

☐ I know what standard my people compare themselves to when they assess their own performance and how they adopted that standard.

☐ I regularly help my people stretch their points of comparison to be something greater.

☐ I challenge the foundations of my own beliefs.

☐ I understand and utilize the power of autopilot.

☐ I help people belong by using insider language.

☐ I help people belong by rituals.

☐ I have clearly identified the enemy for my team to fight, and I speak of that enemy regularly.

☐ I understand my people's reasons for working.

## Chapter 5  Your First 30 Days as Boss

☐ I have decisively identified and removed non-performers.

☐ I have conducted interviews with all of the other department heads to understand how they view my team.

☐ I've asked for the opinions of the support staff and company receptionist.

☐ I've met with at least ten customers in the last 45 days.

☐ I use technology to take notes of all meetings, interviews, and coaching sessions and can review past sessions easily.

☐ I actively rank my salespeople by future potential.

☐ I have a plan for the future state of my team.

☐ I've reviewed my plan with an outside mentor.

☐ I've reviewed my plan with my company boss.

☐ I have buy-in on my plan.

☐ I've shared my vision with the team in a way that left them inspired and ready to act.

☐ I have data and a story to tell that animates the data.

## Chapter 6  Understanding the Market for Hiring

☐ I am successful at hiring superstars 90 percent of the time.
☐ I can clearly define what an A-player is.

## Chapter 7  Step by Step to Hiring a Sales Superstar

☐ My sales job postings describe the ideal person, not the job.
☐ I have a full pipeline of potential hires on reserve just in case I need to hire.
☐ I have a clearly defined hiring process that consistently identifies the best talent.
☐ I conduct pressure interviews skillfully.
☐ I conduct performance interviews skillfully.
☐ I am able to romance and win when I offer jobs to the best candidates.
☐ I research all candidates online.

## Chapter 8  Use the Power of Science in Selection

☐ I use a scientific assessment pre-hire.
☐ I conduct thorough reference checks.

## Chapter 9  On-Boarding a New Member of the Sales Team

☐ I have a structured on-boarding process.
☐ I impress new hires on the first day by the welcome they receive.
☐ I never abandon a salesperson in HR the first day.
☐ I take care of the new hire's family's feelings.
☐ I involve new hires in selling activities on day one.
☐ I role play each stage of the sales process with a new hire.
☐ I assign ride-alongs for new hires with a learning agenda.
☐ I assign new hires to teach at sales meetings right away.
☐ I test for knowledge retention regularly.

☐ I have a formal learning path that lasts a minimum of three years.

☐ I have an automated and digital training library.

☐ I have a dashboard devoted to measured learning.

☐ I have a clear sales process.

☐ One hundred percent of my team would write out the same process if asked.

☐ I have clear outcome measures and stories attached to each step in the sales process.

☐ I have structured sales expectations that allow for individual expression.

☐ I use numbers to identify symptoms, not to diagnose sales problems.

☐ I actively work to minimize the required paperwork my team must complete.

## Chapter 10  Know Your Sales Process and Your Numbers

☐ I have a well-defined sales process.

☐ I know my team's critical numbers.

☐ I know the numbers on a person-by-person basis.

☐ My team has clearly defined quotas.

☐ My team has developed a sales plan to reach their quota.

☐ I know the absolute closing percentage for each of my salespeople.

☐ I know what the fallout is at each stage of our pipeline.

☐ I have a good sense of the prospecting activity that happens on a daily basis.

☐ I know the velocity expected through each stage of the sales process.

☐ I have established a target pipeline value for each person.

☐ My salespeople know how daily behaviors relate to their sales numbers.

☐ My salespeople have an understanding of their "get out of bed" numbers.

☐ I am able to consistently be proactive when identifying current behavior that impacts future sales results.

## Chapter 11 Who Gets My Time and Attention?

☐ I spend most of my time with my superstars.

☐ My superstars feel appreciated.

☐ My superstars view me as their agent removing obstacles.

☐ I challenge my stars' view of their greatness.

☐ I provide rewards in the form of outside training experiences that are not related to sales and that are only available to the very top performers.

☐ I don't tolerate people without sales DNA on the team (cats).

## Chapter 12 Team Rhythms That Lead to Group Cohesion

☐ I let my team vote twice per year on my effectiveness with the meetings I ask them to participate in.

☐ I hold effective meetings.

☐ I have a weekly team check-in.

☐ I have not missed the weekly group check-in meeting for the last 90 days.

☐ I have a structured start to the weekly group check-in that reinforces sales behaviors and results.

☐ I start and end every meeting on time.

☐ I have a monthly roundtable to offer training.

☐ I haven't missed the roundtable in six months.

☐ I have used role play during the roundtable inside of the last 90 days.

☐ I have video-recorded role plays and delivered the results to the team members for review.

☐ I have invited outside parties to our roundtable from other areas of the company in the last 90 days.

☐ I use movie clips, music, and humor during the roundtable.

☐ The team leaves the roundtable energized, motivated, and ready to sell.

☐ I have a well-planned yearly sales team meeting.

☐ I leave plenty of unstructured time at the yearly sales meeting to allow time for members of the team to bond.

☐ I plan for physical activities at the yearly meeting.

☐ I spend money on accommodations so the team feels valued.

## Chapter 13  Individual Rhythms That Lead to Star Performances

☐ I regularly assess individual behavior.

☐ I regularly assess individual outlook.

☐ I regularly assess individual skill.

☐ I regularly assess individual stature.

☐ I hold individual monthly pipeline reviews.

☐ I haven't changed, skipped, or rescheduled a pipeline meeting in the last six months.

☐ I limit wishy-washy explanations from the salesperson.

☐ I gain commitments during pipeline meetings.

☐ I know how to apply increasing pressure as needed.

☐ I resist the urge to ask about the pipeline outside of the formal monthly pipeline review.

☐ I regularly coach specifics on selling skills and processes.

☐ I have role played with every one of my salespeople in the last 60 days.

- ☐ I have monthly planned coaching sessions with each salesperson.
- ☐ I am a master at using reflective listening techniques.
- ☐ I use involved recognition as part of my coaching.
- ☐ I use an established format for coaching.
- ☐ I have video-recorded myself during a coaching session and asked for feedback.
- ☐ I have done a field ride-along with every salesperson in the last six months.
- ☐ I occasionally take the lead on a sales call and allow the salesperson to observe and learn.
- ☐ I identify in advance for the salesperson what skill I am planning to demonstrate on the sales call.
- ☐ I am able to be a silent observer on a sales call and avoid the need to "rescue" the call.
- ☐ I provide immediate and skillful feedback after a ride-along.
- ☐ I keep a record of feedback given and training needed.
- ☐ I tag team sales calls when needed to help close deals, but don't make it a habit.
- ☐ I have done at least two unannounced sales ride-alongs in the last six months.
- ☐ I informally check in by phone or in person with each team member every week.

## Chapter 14  Keep Score Publicly; Motivate Individually

- ☐ I know what metrics drive sales.
- ☐ My team understands the metrics.
- ☐ I post publicly our team and individual sales results and metrics on a daily basis for the company to see.
- ☐ I have identified precise motivators for each member of the team.
- ☐ I use negative motivation sparingly but effectively.

## Chapter 15  Lead by Principle, Not Policy

☐ I lead by principle rather than policies.

☐ I address problems one-on-one rather than create more policies.

☐ My people are able to have a work-life balance.

## Chapter 16  Make Sales Technology Work for You

☐ I have 100 percent compliance from the team in using the CRM daily.

☐ I spend less than one hour each day on average inside the CRM system.

☐ I understand how to get meaningful data out of the CRM system.

☐ I don't ask my team for things they've already reported in the CRM.

☐ I use email to transmit information, but not as a substitute for personal contact or when I am offering guidance or correction.

☐ I don't coach via email.

☐ I don't have a habit of using CC or Reply All on emails.

☐ My team has discussed and agreed on how to use email efficiently.

☐ I use a group messaging service such as Slack or Chatter to help the team stay informed.

☐ I strive to get to the bottom of my email inbox each day.

☐ I use and teach good digital housekeeping skills to the team.

## Chapter 17  Money Talks

☐ I defend the paychecks of my team.

☐ I don't overpay for talent.

☐ I have had a formal compensation study completed when setting pay scales.

☐ My compensation plan allows me to compete for the best talent.

☐ My compensation plan is easy to understand and administer.

☐ My compensation plan is tied to things that are under the direct control of the salesperson.

☐ There is a wide range in level of compensation between the bottom and the top performers.

☐ My salespeople could never live their chosen lifestyles on the base salary.

☐ I always issue the compensation plan prior to the start of the new year.

☐ I pay variable and bonus compensation as close as possible to the time of sale, rather than when the company collects payment.

☐ I have a dashboard that allows my salespeople to understand what they are owed and from which customers their variable comp has been paid.

☐ I don't reserve house accounts.

## Chapter 18  Forecasting the Future

☐ I am able to forecast confidently and with accuracy.

☐ The executive team knows they can count on my forecast.

☐ My salespeople participate in creating the forecast.

☐ I am willing to defend my forecast numbers rather than raise them arbitrarily.

## Chapter 19  Replicating Success

☐ I engage in territory planning to ensure proper coverage of all target prospects.

☐ I've identified our ideal targets.

☐ I've facilitated the formation of parallel sales groups for the exchange of leads.

☐ I work to help my team position themselves as experts through speaking and writing opportunities.

## Chapter 20 The Business of You

☐ I view myself as an entrepreneur.

☐ I am mentally healthy and balance my stress.

☐ I am physically healthy.

☐ I control my use of alcohol.

☐ I have attended a non-work-related conference in the last year for enjoyment and learning.

☐ I read widely outside my industry.

☐ I read widely in my industry.

☐ I have sacred personal time.

☐ I have sacred family time.

☐ I know how to relax and rejuvenate myself.

☐ I have a mentor.

☐ I understand the secret.

☐ I am the Sales Boss.

# About the Author

**Jonathan Whistman** is a Partner at the consulting firm Elevate Human Potential (www.elevatehp.com). His work is centered on the belief that the greatest business results come from focusing on elevating the human potential within a business. When companies are able to tap into the imagination, talent, and vision of their people, they see a dramatic increase in sales and a reduced level of workplace stress. Elevate Human Potential has helped build the sales teams of hundreds of companies ranging in size from $1 to $250 million in annual revenue. Jonathan has personally observed over 2,500 individual sales calls and uses these insights to help develop selling strategies and management practices that lead teams to selling success.

Jonathan brings his unique insights shaped from both his childhood and business experiences to his consulting work. He was raised in a family with eight kids, and his childhood was spent inside a religious cult, where he devoted over 10,000 hours knocking on doors to create radical conversions in lifestyles and belief in the lives of those he called on. In addition, he became a leader, regularly giving inspirational and instructional talks to audiences of up to 11,000 people. This up-close look at how people form, change, and develop beliefs became a foundation for understanding how to lead organizations and sales teams where success depends on getting the power of belief ignited in the people you lead or the customers you sell to.

Leaving the beliefs of his childhood forced him to become familiar with the challenges that come from overcoming an ingrained way of thinking and being. Using these insights, Jonathan has trained, hired, managed, observed, and coached thousands of salespeople through his work with leading sales organizations that also must overcome habits, beliefs, and challenges that stand in the way of the highest level of success. He has been instrumental in molding the leadership talents of countless companies. His own companies have been featured on CNN Money, have won the GEW Top 50 High Growth companies' designation, and achieved the SXSW Top 5 Award. When not working, he enjoys long-distance backpacking, motorcycling, and reading. He recently completed a 540-mile hike across Spain with Kellie Zimmet, the love of his life and business partner. His greatest business satisfaction comes from enabling a CEO or business owner to feel like he or she has their life back when the team is running well and achieving at the highest level, and from seeing people overcome their own beliefs that restrict their potential. His greatest personal satisfaction comes in knowing he was able to change his own beliefs and thus create a better life for himself and his son.

You can reach Jonathan at jon@elevatehp.com.

# Index

Absolute closing percentage from quota, 130
Accepting fault mindset, 27–28
Accountability, 185
Active engagement, 23–24
Adamson, Brent, 137
"Always already listening," 166–167
Amazon Fulfillment Centers, 41
American Dream, 32
Analytical minds, 20–21
Apple, 43–44, 86
Assessment tools: Everything DiSC, 106, 107–108; PXT Select, 106–107; used during the hiring process, 105–106
Authenticity: characteristics of, 25; how to fire someone with, 48–49; inspiring loyalty and respect through, 21; skills and process coaching with, 168; of your first communication with team, 50
Authority: lead by principles approach to, 191–193; why firing a sales team member is a show of, 48–49
Autopilot behavior, 37, 39
Awesome Anomaly (high-earners): description of a, 17; why they don't make good Sales Bosses, 17–18

Base salary compensation, 210
Behavior: accurate forecasting requires understanding of your buyers', 223; autopilot, 37, 39; individual meeting BOSS framework on, 156; jealous reaction to paychecks of top performers, 207; ten truths of human behavior, 32–39; weekly group check-in meetings and comparing sales, 146
Behavior styles: benefits of sales team variety of, 108; Everything DiSC assessment of, 106, 107–108; PXT Select assessment of communication and, 106–107
Behavior truths: 1: things are only good or bad by comparison, 32–35, 39; 2: people believe they are giving 100 percent or have reason not to, 35–36, 39; 3: people love autopilot, 37, 39; 4: people need to belong, 37–38, 39; 5: the only reasons that matter are their reasons, 38–39
Beliefs: believe bigger mindset, 27; of people that they are giving 100 percent, 35–36, 39; and understanding of what "great" is, 33
Belonging: having a common enemy to reinforce, 42–44; need for, 37–38, 39; rituals to reinforce, 41–42, 63; unique insider language to reinforce, 40–41, 63
Big fish in small pond, 34
Bonuses: cash or non-cash incentives used for, 211, 217; limit number of items measured for, 215
Bradberry, Travis, 19
The buck stops here, 27–28

Camtasia, 119
The Challenger Sale (Dixon and Adamson), 137
Chatter, 200
Claure, Marcelo, 43
Coaching. See Skills and process coaching
Comcast's compensation plan disaster, 209–210
Commissions: base salary and/or, 210; variable, 211, 214
Common enemy, 42–44
Communication: "always already listening" approach to, 166–167; first introduction to team as the manager, 49–50; group-messaging tool used for, 201; language of helping, 186–187; PXT Select assessment of an individual's approach to, 106–107; unique insider language used in group, 40–41, 63; words to use for skills and process coaching, 165–166. See also Emails; Feedback
Communication style, 150
Companies: on-boarding and training new hires, 111–122; providing new hires with best impression of your, 113–114; reducing turnover rates, 112–114
Compensation: cash or non-cash incentives as, 211, 217; ERI studies on, 208; job posting with realistic earning figure and expectation, 80; make sure you aren't overpaying a sales team member, 207–208; observation on jealous reactions of others to top performers,' 207; TTC (total target compensation), 212–213; verifying job candidate's earnings claim, 80–81; W-2 forms to verify a job candidate's claimed, 80–81, 208
Compensation plan best practices: don't change plans mid-year or suddenly, 213–214; issue the plan before the time period it covers, 214; limit number of items measured for variable commissions or bonuses, 215; Pavlov dog principle for paying variable comp, 214; post how compensation is calculated on the dashboard, 214–215
Compensation plans: on base salary, 210; best practices for, 213–215; on bonuses, 211, 215, 217; cash or other non-cash incentives, 211; check for any unintended consequences of your, 209; Comcast's cautionary story on a faulty, 209–210; on "house accounts," 215–216; knowing how much "a lot of money" is factor of, 213; on paying on consumables or parts sales, 216; top four things that must be true about any, 209; on variable commissions, 211, 214, 215
Conferences, 235–236
Consumables or parts sales, 216
Crestcom Leadership, 144
Customer relationship management (CRM) systems: adding automation for role-playing sales scenarios, 120; data

256

analytics using the, 58–60; having penalties in place for not using, 197–198; how companies utilize their, 5; minimum features of an up-to-date, 198–200; pipeline performance reviews and, 158, 161; public posting of scores using the, 183–184; salesforce.com solutions for, 199; training new hires on your, 115; understanding human behavior versus depending on, 31. *See also* Sales numbers; Sales technology

Customer story, 127–128

Customers: accurate forecasting requires understanding behavior of your, 223; house accounts with, 215–216; meeting them during first 30–day period, 57–58; training new hires using sales activity with, 115–116; writing the story of your, 127–128. *See also* Prospects

Dashboards: for accountability and to leverage productive changes, 185; hold meetings with it visible, 184–185; listing all metrics relevant to your team scores, 183; post how compensation is calculated on, 214–215; using the CRM tool for public posting of, 183–184. *See also* Sales numbers

Day one tasks: force rank your sales team, 61–62; review your meeting notes, 61; visualizing how to organize your team, 62–63

Day two tasks: articulate your sales plan, 63; share your plans and ask for feedback, 63–64

Day three tasks: list the critical activities to focus on, 67; meeting with the salesperson that is to be let go, 66–67; planning your presentation of the sales plan, 64–66; write your 90–day to-do list, 66

Decision making: one-third plus one technique for actionable items, 144–145; trusting their team to make good, 191–192; on which sales team member to fire, 47–48

Dixon, Matthew, 137

Dread Private Roberts story, 149–150

Earnings. *See* Compensation

Emails: etiquette and rules for using and organizing, 201–202; sent to frame ten-minute phone screening expectations, 93–94; using Chatter or Slack alternatives for internal, 200; as a valuable sales tool, 200. *See also* Communication

*Emotional intelligence 2.0* (Bradberry and Greaves), 19

Emotional intelligence (EQ): description and three skills of, 19; individual meetings and value of your, 155; research on relationship of earnings to, 19–20

Entrepreneur mindset: attending non-work-related conference or training, 235–236; getting the right mentor as part of a, 239–240; importance of having a, 235; increasing your reading diet as part of a, 236

ERI compensation studies, 208

Evernote: keeping organized with, 57–58; review your meeting notes on, 61

Everything DiSC: description of, 106; the science behind, 107–108

FAB: feature-advantage-benefit, 118

Fall-out numbers, between each stage leading to close, 130

Families: "Thanks for leading us your spouse" package for, 114; yearly sales gathering inclusion of, 152

Feedback: delivering bad, 168–169; *involved recognition*, 169–170; praise as, 20; ride-alongs and, 171–179; on your sales plan, 63–64. *See also* Communication

File-naming convention system, 202–203

Firing: meeting with the salesperson to be let go, 66–67; a sales team member during first 30–day period, 47–49; as show of authority, 48–49; visualizing what sales team members might need, 63. *See also* Hiring

First 30–day period: data analytics using your CRM system, 58–60; deciding which member of your sales team to fire, 47–49; gathering information on the company and sales team, 51–57; introducing yourself to the sales team, 49–50; meeting your customers during the, 57–58; take a working three-day vacation tasks, 60–61–67

*Forbes* magazine, 236

Forecasting: as the bane of existence for most sales managers, 221; challenges related to accurate, 221–222; data-driven and thoughtful process of accurate, 223–224; "if nothing changes, then nothing changes" secret of accurate, 222–223, 224; understanding your buyers' behavior for accurate, 223. *See also* Sales numbers

Fractivity tradition, 40–41

"Funeral managing," 138

Galen, 105

Good or bad by comparison: how people define "great" example of, 33–34; setting yearly sales goal example of, 34–35; story of woman's resilience and viewpoint example of, 32; understanding the human behavior principle of, 32–35, 39

Google, 86

"Great" standards, 33–35

Greaves, Jean, 19

Group-messaging tool, 201

Groups: having a common enemy, 42–44; need of individuals to belong to a, 37–38, 39; rituals of, 41–42, 63; unique insider language of, 40–41, 63. *See also* Individuals

Health habits: do regular check-ins on your self-care and, 240; honest assessment of your, 241; setting aside family "sacred time," 238–239; setting aside personal "sacred time," 236–238; take time for effective relaxation, 239; what your personal appearance reveals about your, 240–241

Helping language, 186–187

Hiring: challenges of superstar salesperson, 71–75; understanding that an unemployed salesperson is a red flag, 72; understanding that great salespeople are seldom available for, 72; why a super salesperson might be available for, 73–74. *See also* Firing; On-boarding

Hiring process: assessment tools used during the, 105–108; design a well-written job posting, 79–85; dissecting the résumé, 86–88; interviewing during the, 88–101; reaching out to targeted people during the, 85–86

Honesty, 24

House accounts, 215–216

Human behavior. *See* Behavior

Individual meeting BOSS framework: Behavior component, 156; Outlook component, 156–157; Skills component, 157; Stature component, 157

Individual meeting types: pipeline performance review, 158–161; skills and process coaching, 161–180

Individual meetings: BOSS framework for, 156–157; management code and mindset to have at, 155–156; three types of, 158–180

Individuals: five fundamental truths about human behavior of, 31–39; importance of understanding, 31. *See also* Groups

Information: caution about how to best use gathered, 56–57; support staff as source of, 53–56

Interview 4-stage process: 1: the ten-minute phone screening, 90–94; 2: the pressure interview, 94–98, 128; 3: the performance interview, 99–100; 4: the romance interview, 100–101, 128

Interviewing: adopting a polite but direct mindset for, 89–90; examining the process of, 88–89; the four-stage interview process, 89–101
*Involved recognition* feedback, 169–170

Jazz club metaphor, 11–12
Job candidates: dissecting the résumé of, 86–88; interviewing, 88–101; request example of recent selling success by, 81–82; understanding that an unemployed salesperson is a red flag, 72; understanding that great salespeople are seldom available as, 72; verify their earnings with a W-2 form, 80–81, 208; why a super salesperson might be available as a, 73–74
Job posting: describe industries and experience preferences in, 81; emphasis on *type of person* in the, 84; example of a well-written, 82–84; example of recent selling success request in the, 81–82; identify what skills are required, 79–80; include realistic earning figure and expectation, 80; where to post your, 84–85
Jobs, Steve, 43–44
Judgment of others, 21–22

Kouzes, Jim, 159

Language of helping, 186–187
Lead by principles, 191–193
*The Leadership Challenge* (Kouzes and Posner), 159
Learning management systems (LMSs), 120
Learning rides: description of the, 172; example of a successful, 173–174; how to prepare for an effective, 173
Legere, John, 43
Life-work balance: do regular check-ins on your, 240; setting aside family "sacred time" for, 238–239; setting aside personal "sacred time" for, 236–238; take time for effective relaxation, 239; what your personal appearance reveals about your, 240–241
LinkedIn, 86, 231
Listening: "always already," 166–167; clarifying and reflective, 167–168
Loyalty, a great Sales Boss inspires, 21

Mac versus PC commercials, 43
Management: the code of management to guide, 22–28, 155; lead by principle rather than rules, 191–193. *See also* Sacred Rhythms; Sales managers
Management Code: applied to individual meetings, 155; be authentic; people are people, 22, 25; be the thermostat, not the thermometer, 22, 25–26; believe bigger, 23, 27; don't micro-manage; be actively engaged, 22, 23–24; the fault is always mine, 23, 27–28; honesty always; no one should ever be surprised, 22, 24; overview of the, 22–23; trust and expect the best, but verify, 22, 26–27
Massie, Suzanne, 26
Meetings: "have-a-minute?," 180; individual and ride-alongs, 155–180. *See also* Sales meetings
Mentors, 239–240
Micro-managing: be actively engaged instead of, 23–24; how an automated training system prevents problem of, 121–122
Mindmarker, 121
Mindsets: accepting fault, 27–28; believe bigger, 27; entrepreneur, 235–240; for holding individual meetings, 155–156; interviewing with a polite but direct, 89–90
*Mission Impossible* (TV show), 126
Monthly roundtable meetings: Dread Pirate Roberts story on setting the right tone, 149–150; recommended strategies to use during, 148–149; relaxed tone and focus of the, 147; selecting different rhythms to use during, 148

Motivation: centered on teaching and caretaking, 186; creating a selling environment that encourages, 187; dashboards not used just for, 185; how to discover people's true, 185–187; language of helping to add to people's, 186–187; need for recognition as, 185–186; negative, 187–188; understanding sales team members and *their* reasons driving, 38–39

Negative motivation, 187–188
Non-work-related conference or training, 235–236
Norms: how rituals reinforce, 41–42, 63; how unique insider language reinforces, 40–41, 63. *See also* Sales culture

On-boarding: example of poorly done, 112–113; example of well-done, 113–114; get your new person in and out of HR quickly, 111; impression of your company determined during, 114–115; strategies for inserting sales activity throughout, 115–116; "visas" stamped in passports to new hires during, 122. *See also* Hiring; Training
One-third plus one technique, 144–145
Outlook (BOSS framework), 156–157

Parts or consumables sales, 216
PC versus Mac commercials, 43
Performance: challenges of forecasting, 221–224; connecting skills and process coaching to, 163–164; dashboards used to leverage productive change in, 185
The performance interview: conducting a role-play and give feedback during, 100; conducting background screening prior to the, 100; how to ask for the candidate's participation in, 99–100; purpose of the, 99
Performance metrics: how standards of "great" impact, 33–35; principle of comparison for setting, 34–35; trust but verify, 26–27
Pipeline performance reviews: actions to take or not take following the, 160–161; the CRM used during but not substituted for, 158, 161; description and monthly schedule of, 158; focus on accuracy of salesperson's forecasts during, 159–160; sales quotas and targets discussion during, 158–159; upcoming meetings with prospects topic of, 159
Posner, Barry, 159
Praise: great sales managers don't need, 20; management role to give advice and, 20
The pressure interview: format to use for the, 95–98; a pressure exercise for the candidate during the, 98; timing allowed for the, 94–95; what the name reminds you of, 128
Principles: lead not by rules but by, 191–193; Sacred Rhythms versus, 193
Professional development: attending non-work-related conference or training for, 235–236; getting the right mentor for, 239–240; increasing your reading diet for, 236. *See also* Self-care; Training
Prospecting numbers: description of the, 130; to understand efforts related to prospecting, 133–134
Prospects: coaching by taking ride-alongs to see, 171–178; contact numbers to understand efforts related to, 133–134; pipeline performance review on upcoming meetings with, 159; sales number of contacts made to, 130, 159–160. *See also* Customers
PXT Select, 106–107

Quota: absolute closing percentage from the, 130; knowing total target sales revenue number from the, 130
Quota stage: absolute closing percentage from, 130; knowing the total target sales revenue number during, 130

Recognition: *involved recognition* feedback, 169–170; motivation through need for, 185–186

Reflective listening, 167–168

Regan, Ronald, 26

Religious cult: author's experience growing up in a, 6; "religious sales teams" of, 6–7

Replicating success: territory planning strategy for, 228–231; by understanding what needs to happen for, 227–228

Resilience, 32

Respect: sales manager's ability to inspire natural, 21; your team's ability to make good decisions, 191–192

Résumés: match them to a specific type of sales job, 87–88; patterns to watch out for, 88; three-pile method for reviewing submitted, 87

Retention rates: example of well-done on-boarding to reduce, 113–114; how poor on-boarding practices contribute to, 112–113

Ride-alongs: benefits of effective, 179; following up with role-playing scenarios, 179; getting the most value out of, 171–172; the learning ride, 172–174; the silent observer, 174–176, 179; tag team, 176; unannounced, 176–178

Rituals: examples of company, 41–42; identifying your sales team, 63; sense of belonging through, 41

Role playing: Customer relationship management (CRM) system and automated, 120; following up live ride-alongs with, 179; as a practice drill, 163; skills and process coaching use of, 162–163

The romance interview: "giving the new boss a ride" during, 101; the purpose of the, 100–101; what the name reminds you of, 128

Sacred Rhythms: description and importance of establishing, 12–14; establishing ongoing training as a, 121–122; first 30-day period task of firing someone and implementing new, 48; for managing meetings, 143–152; visualize what you want to implement in your team, 63. *See also* Management; Sales Bosses; Sales culture; Sales teams

Sale managers: typically spend the most time on underperformers, 137–138; why a higher-earner (Awesome Anomaly) doesn't make a good, 17–18. *See also* Management; Sales Bosses

Sale stage: absolute closing percentage from quote, 130; exercise on defining each episode or, 127–128; fall-out number between each of the, 130; knowing the numbers that matter during, 129–134; number of prospecting contacts during, 130, 133–134; target pipeline value expectation during, 130; total target sales revenue number, 130; understanding the fall-out between stages, 131–132; velocity of each, 130, 132–133

Sales activities: learning expectations and testing on training, 117–118; planning and setting high standard for training, 116; training new hires using, 115–116

Sales Boss Scorecard: Chapter 1, 243; Chapter 2, 244; Chapter 3, 244; Chapter 4, 244–245; Chapter 5, 245; Chapters 6 through 8, 246; Chapter 9, 246–247; Chapter 10, 247; Chapter 11, 248; Chapter 12, 248–249; Chapter 13, 249–250; Chapter 14, 250; Chapter 15, 250; Chapter 16, 251; Chapter 17, 251–252; Chapter 18, 252; Chapter 19, 252; Chapter 20, 253

Sales Bosses: communication style of effective, 150; the DNA of a great, 17–28; emotional intelligence (EQ) of, 19–20, 155; the first 30 days as a, 47–67; having an entrepreneur mindset and effective self-care, 235–241; lead by principle rather than rules, 191–193; Management Code of great, 22–27, 155; understanding the *what* and importance of job done by, 3–8. *See also* Sacred Rhythms; Sales managers

Sales Bosses DNA: 1: they have sales role but not as top performer, 17–19; 2: they have a high level of emotional intelligence (EQ), 19–20; 3: they don't need the credit to feed their egos, 20; 4: they have balanced analytical minds, 20–21; 5: they inspire loyalty and can hold the attention of a room, 21; 6: they are comfortable sitting in judgment, 21–22

Sales culture: crafting an environment that reinforces high expectations, 38; how the "Fractivity" tradition reinforced a, 40–41; jazz club metaphor of the, 11–12; leveraging the need to belong in a, 37–38; the rhythm and energy of the, 11–12; rituals of your, 41–42, 63. *See also* Norms; Sacred Rhythms; Selling environment

Sales issues analysis: caution about using gathered information for, 56; getting information from the support staff for, 52–56; questions to ask for your, 54–56

Sales managers: forecasting as the bane of existence for most, 221; micro-managing by, 23–24, 121–122; why a higher-earner (Awesome Anomaly) doesn't make a good, 17–18. *See also* Management; Sales Bosses

Sales meetings: during the first 30-day discovery period, 51; having an open discussion on improving, 143–145; held with the dashboard visible, 184–185; monthly roundtable, 147–150; one-third plus one technique for actionable items during, 144–145; review your notes on past, 61; video-record several of your, 168; voting twice yearly on whether to keep, 143; weekly group check-in, 145–147; yearly sales gathering, 151–152

Sales numbers: absolute closing percentage from quote, 130; fall-out number between each stage, 130; a few words of caution about, 129; number of prospecting contacts made, 130, 133–134, 159–160; pipeline performance review of the, 159–160; target pipeline value expectation, 130; understanding the metrics driving individual and group, 130; understanding the ones that matter, 129–134; velocity of each stage, 130, 132–133; weekly group check-in meeting focus on key metric, 146–147. *See also* Customer relationship management (CRM) systems; Dashboards; Forecasting

Sales plans: articulate your, 63; data analytics to help form your, 58–60; gathering information to help organize your, 51–57; share it with other and ask for feedback, 63–64

Sales processes: comparing a successful TV series to, 125–126, 127–128; define each episode/stage exercise on, 127–128; importance of knowing your, 125; lack of agreement on steps of the, 126–127; writing out a customer story as part of your, 127–128

Sales stage: absolute closing percentage from quote, 130; exercise on defining each episode or, 127–128; fall-out number between each of the, 130; knowing the numbers that matter during, 129–134; number of prospecting contacts during, 130, 133–134; target pipeline value expectation during, 130; total target sales revenue number, 130; understanding the fall-out between stages, 131–132; velocity of each, 130, 132–133

Sales team members: benefits of having variety of behavior styles among, 108; caring less about company goals and more about the, 39; crafting an environment that reinforces high expectations of, 38; deciding which one to fire, 47–49; discovering their true motivation, 185–187; don't keep a C-player ("cat"), 140; force rank your, 61–62; huge gap between a superstar salesperson and the average, 137; impact of bad hiring of a, 13; jealous reaction to paychecks of superstars by other, 207; on-boarding a new, 111–122; understanding *their* reasons of individual, 38–39; understanding *their* reasons, 38–39. *See also* Superstar salespersons; Underperforming salespersons

Sales teams: Awesome Anomaly (high-earners) among, 17–18; being the thermostat of your, 25–26; believe bigger than your, 27; benefits of having variety of behavior styles in, 108; first communication as sales manager to your, 49–50; a great Sales Boss inspires loyalty of the, 21; having a common enemy, 42–44; how bad hiring decisions impact, 13; how standards of "great" impact performance of, 33–35; leading by principle rather than rules, 191–193; outlining the plan for your, 62–63; positioning them as experts, 230–231; rituals of your, 41–42, 63; unique insider language of your, 40–41, 63. *See also* Sacred Rhythms

Sales technology: communicating to your team the benefits of, 197; email as a valuable, 200–202; file-naming convention for shared documents, 202–203; group-messaging tool, 201; having penalties in place for not using, 197–198; Twitter feed used for client projects, 200–201. *See also* Customer relationship management (CRM) systems

salesforce.com, 199

Scores. *See* Dashboards

Self-care: do regular check-ins on your, 240; setting aside family "sacred time" for, 238–239; setting aside personal "sacred time" for, 236–238; take time for effective relaxation, 239; what your personal appearance reveals about your, 240–241

Selling: experience with "religious sales teams," 6–7; job posting request to provide recent experience in, 81–82

Selling environment: creating one that encourages action and motivation, 187; Great Sales Success + Mediocre Environment = Great Sales Person, 75; providing superstar salespersons with the best, 74–75. *See also* Sales culture

Servant leaders, 21

Silent observer rides: description and purpose of a, 174–175; doing a minimum of two per year, 179; two examples of an effective, 175–176

Skills and process coaching: agenda for a typical session, 170–171; "always already listening" impact on, 166–167; with authenticity, 168; being "present" when engaged in, 161–162; connecting performance to, 163–164; delivering bad news when, 168–169; effective ride-alongs to include with, 171–179; *involved recognition* during, 169–170; one-to-one, 161; reflective listening and clarifying during, 167–168; role playing during your, 162–163; using fear and authority sparingly for, 164–165; video-record some of your, 168; weekly informal check-in via phone, 179–180; words and language to use for, 165–166

Skills (BOSS framework), 157

Slack, 200

Sprint, 43

*Star Wars* (TV show), 126

Stature (BOSS framework), 157

Superstar salespersons: being an agent and ally to your, 138–140; challenges of hiring a, 71–75; designing a well-written job posting for, 79–85; dissecting their résumé, 86–88; doing a minimum of two silent observer rides with, 179; don't make mistake of a hands-off approach to, 138; ensure that your compensation plan won't drive away a, 209; as few and always in demand, 72; huge gap between an average salesperson and a, 137; interviewing a prospective, 89–101; jealous reaction to paychecks of, 207; providing them with the best selling environment, 74–75; why one might be unemployed or looking elsewhere, 73–74. *See also* Sales team members

Support staff: always be nice to the, 53; as great source of information, 53–56; questions to ask the, 54–56

*Survivor* (TV show), 126

T-Mobile, 43

Tag team ride-alongs, 176

Target pipeline value expectation, 130

Ten-minute phone screening: brief description of the, 90; email invite to frame expectations for performance, 93–94; rating responses given during the, 92–93; script used for, 90–92

Termination. *See* Firing

Territory planning: description and benefits of, 228–229; example of how it works, 229–230; positioning your team as experts as part of, 230–231; replicating success using, 228–231

Thermostat metaphor, 25–26

Three-day working vacation: benefits of scheduling a, 60–61; day one tasks during your, 61–63

Tony Robbins–style seminar, 139

Total target sales revenue number, 130

Training: attending non-work-related, 235–236; benefits of role-playing sales scenarios using CRM systems, 120; establishing ongoing training as a Sacred Rhythm, 121–122; learning expectations and testing on sales activities during, 117–118; learning management systems (LMSs) for, 120; staggering learning expectations and testing during, 116–118; strategies for inserting sales activity throughout on-boarding, 115–116; video-recording to build training library for, 118–120; "visas" stamped in passports to new hires during, 122. *See also* On-boarding; Professional development

Training library: Camtasia recommended for creating content for, 119; importance of having a, 118; video-recording in order to stock your, 118–120

Training products: Camtasia, 119; Mindmarker's, 121

Travel budgets, 191–192

Trust: how honesty builds, 24; "trust but verify" approach to, 26–27; in your team's ability to make good decisions, 191–192

TTC (total target compensation), 212–213

Turnover rates: example of well-done on-boarding to reduce, 113–114; how poor on-boarding practices contribute to, 112–113

TV series metaphor, 125–126, 127–128

Twitter feed, 200–201

Unannounced ride-alongs: description of a, 176–177; example of an effective, 177–178; the goal of these, 177

Underperforming salespersons: accusations of micro-managing by, 24; don't keep a C-player ("cat"), 140; sales managers typically spend the most time on, 137–138. *See also* Sales team members

Unique insider language, 40–41, 63

Variable commissions: description of, 211; limit number of items measured for, 215; pay as close to the pay period as possible, 214

Velocity of stages: description and meaning of the, 132; importance of knowing the, 130; knowing when a deal is over or unlikely using the, 132–133

Video-recording: some sales meetings and coaching sessions, 168; of training to build training library, 118–120

W-2 form verification, 80, 208

Weekly group check-in meetings: best day to hold, 145–146; key guidelines for holding the, 147; key metric to add to check-in during, 146–147; three sections of an effective, 146–147

Yearly sales gatherings: description and focus of the, 151; setting aside time for bonding and interactions, 151–152

YouTube CRM systems video, 199

CPSIA information can be obtained
at www.ICGtesting.com
Printed in the USA
LVHW081111091022
730252LV00023B/101

9 781119 286646